The Struggle for Equality

Women and Minorities in America

Spring Hermann

 Enslow Publishers, Inc.

40 Industrial Road
Box 398
Berkeley Heights, NJ 07922
USA

http://www.enslow.com

Library of Congress Cataloging-in-Publication Data

Hermann, Spring.
    The struggle for equality : women and minorities in America /
Spring Hermann.
        p. cm. — (The American saga)
    Includes bibliographical references (p.   ) and index.
    ISBN 0-7660-2573-X
    1. Equality—United States—History—Juvenile literature. 2. Minorities—
Civil rights—United States—History—Juvenile literature. 3. African
Americans—Civil rights—History—Juvenile literature. 4. Women's rights—
United States—History—Juvenile literature. 5. Civil rights movements—
United States—History—Juvenile literature. 6. United States—Race
relations—Juvenile literature. 7. United States—Social conditions—
Juvenile literature. I. Title. II. Series.
HN90.S6H47 2006
323.0973—dc22

                                    2005027234

Printed in the United States of America

10 9 8 7 6 5 4 3 2 1

To Our Readers:
We have done our best to make sure all Internet Addresses in this book were
active and appropriate when we went to press. However, the author and the
publisher have no control over and assume no liability for the material available
on those Internet sites or on other Web sites they may link to. Any comments or
suggestions can be sent by e-mail to comments@enslow.com or to the address on
the back cover.

Illustration Credits: Associated Press/AP, pp. 45, 85; ©Bob
Daemmrich / The Image Works, p. 107; © Corel Corporation, p. 15;
Denver Public Library/Western History Collection, pp. 96, 110 (top);
©Fransisco Rangel / The Image Works, p. 90; Getty Images, pp. 1 (left),
70; ©2003 Jim West/The Image Works, pp. 4, 73; ©Kent Meireis /The
Image Works, p. 83; Library of Congress, pp. 1 (center and right), 6, 8,
24, 25, 28, 32, 35, 42, 52, 53, 55, 56, 59, 62, 69, 78, 88, 100, 109, 110
(bottom), 111, 112, 113; ©Mark Godfrey/The Image Works, p. 66; ©Mary
Evans Picture Library / The Image Works, p. 21; Photo by Michelle
Frankfurter for the U.S. Census Bureau, p. 103; Time Life
Pictures/Getty Images, pp. 41, 46, 92; U.S. Army, p. 39.

Cover Illustration: Library of Congress (inset); Time Life Pictures/
Getty Images (large photo).

Contents

This is the original bus on which Rosa Parks refused to give up her seat. The event sparked the Montgomery bus boycott and helped fuel the civil rights movement of the 1950s and 1960s.

Rosa Parks Worked for Equal Rights

During the summer of 1955, Rosa Parks rode the bus. Her home was in Montgomery, Alabama. She was one of fifty thousand African Americans living in that city. Parks had no car. She needed the bus to get to and from her job. She worked in the tailoring shop of a department store.

Parks also rode the bus to her volunteer job on Thursday evenings with the Youth Council of the National Association for the Advancement of Colored People (NAACP). "Colored people" was a term used then for African Americans. At the Youth Council, Parks counseled teenagers.

One of Parks' teens at the Youth Council was Claudette Colvin, who remembered that "Mrs. Parks said always do what is right."[1] Parks was teaching Claudette to believe in herself. She told her to keep her dignity. Parks was working for the day when African Americans would get respect and equal treatment. That day had not yet come.

Rosa Parks rode the bus in August 1955 to an

Martin Luther King, Jr., gets ready to have a press conference on March 26, 1964.

NAACP meeting. She heard a young minister named Martin Luther King, Jr., speak. Only thirty people made it to hear Dr. King. The pastor talked about a 1954 U.S. Supreme Court decision. It was called *Brown v. Board of Education*. This ruling said that it was against the U.S. Constitution to make African-American children go to separate schools from other children. Parks was impressed with how well King spoke. She said later "he was well prepared to take a role of leadership."[2]

A Famous Bus Ride

On Thursday, December 1, 1955, Rosa Parks headed home from her job. She had been on her feet all day. She was glad to find a seat on the bus. Parks sat in the middle section. Her seat was just behind the sign that read "colored." Alabama law stated that African Americans had to sit in the rear half of a bus or train car. Signs often read, "This part of the bus for the colored race."[3]

Many white people got on Parks' bus. One white

man still needed a seat. The driver ordered Rosa and the three other African Americans to move farther back. The three gave up their seats and moved. Rosa Parks did not.

Parks remembered her grandfather. He told her about the fear he had of white people. He was afraid they would attack his home. Parks made a decision that would change her life; she would never give in to fear again. The driver asked her if she was going to stand up. Parks said: "No."

The driver left the bus to call the police. Parks recalled thinking, "I could be manhandled or beaten. I could be arrested." Two policemen came for her. When Rosa asked, "Why do you all push us around?" the policeman said he did not know, but the law was the law.[4] They drove Parks to the city jail. She was booked and locked in a cell.

Word spread rapidly through the African-American community. Rosa Parks had been arrested! Two lawyers offered to defend her. One was a white man, Clifford Durr. He was the husband of Parks' friend, Virginia Durr, a white woman. The other was Fred Gray, one of two black lawyers in Montgomery.[5] These men knew that Parks would be put on trial. The African Americans of Montgomery quickly joined together. E. D. Nixon, head of the Montgomery chapter of the NAACP, raised Parks' bail.[6]

During that night, while Parks was being bailed out of jail, supporters printed thirty-five thousand handbills. The next day, people took the handbills to every black school in Montgomery. Each student was asked to take one home. The handbill said:

> [I]f Negroes [another name then for African Americans] did not ride the buses, they could not operate. Three-fourths of the riders are Negroes, yet we are arrested, or have to stand over empty seats. . . . We are, therefore, asking every Negro to stay off the buses Monday in protest of the arrest and trial. . . . Please stay off all buses Monday.[7]

The city's African-American ministers asked all of their church members to boycott the buses. This

Rosa Parks is fingerprinted shortly after her arrest.

meant everyone that did so would have to walk to work on Monday.

The Stopping Place for Rosa Parks

Rosa Parks' husband, Raymond, and her mother were frightened. She upset them with her actions. Raymond Parks was in tears when he finally got his wife home. He kept saying, "Rosa, the white folks will kill you."[8]

Parks knew she could be in danger. African Americans who stood up to white people were often hurt. Parks had come to a point in her life where she had to make a stand.

Parks knew that she had many rights that her African-American ancestors never had. She was a free citizen. Her great-grandmother and her grandmother had been born into slavery. Parks had the right to go to school. Her slave ancestors were not even taught to read and write. Parks' mother had a teacher's certificate from Payne University in Selma, Alabama. Parks attended a private high school for African-American girls in Montgomery. However, she was not able to graduate. She had to stop and take care of sick family members. Yet she cherished the education that she had.

Rosa Parks had the legal right to vote. Women before her had fought for this privilege. African-American men and women both had trouble getting registered to vote. Parks had been turned down several times. By 1945, however, she was registered. Parks also had the right to work outside her home. Years before, married women, whether black or white, had no legal right to their own money. The husband controlled the family funds and property. Now Parks could keep her paycheck. These were her many rights.

Why Rosa Parks Was Not Free

Rosa Parks knew she was still not free. The Southern states kept white and black citizens separated from each other in public places. State and city laws said African Americans could not enter waiting rooms, rest

> **"To my mind there was no way you could make segregation decent or nice or acceptable."**
> —Rosa Parks

rooms, restaurants, shops, hotels, theaters, parks, and swimming pools that were labeled "For Whites Only." They could not even take a sip from a "White" drinking fountain. African-American children went to "black only" schools. Their school buildings were almost always badly built. They had few supplies. In the 1954 *Brown v. Board of Education* decision, the U.S. Supreme Court struck down segregated schools.

The segregation law that Rosa Parks deeply resented was the one sending her to the back of the bus. The bus drivers and white passengers were not always rude. However, Parks still felt she was being treated badly. She said, "To my mind there was no way you could make segregation decent or nice or acceptable."[9]

The Montgomery Bus Boycott Succeeds

Almost all of the African Americans in Montgomery boycotted the bus with Rosa Parks. Reverend Martin Luther King, Jr., wrote in his book *Stride Toward Freedom* that he waited that first Monday morning for a bus to pass. No African Americans were aboard. "A miracle had taken place," he would later write of the almost complete participation in the boycott.[10] Rosa Parks walked to her job. Sometimes she rode in a car pool. Eventually, she was fired. She started to receive threats. Still, Parks continued to fight for civil rights.

Other African Americans stayed off the buses no matter the weather. Bus drivers had forced African Americans to enter the rear door of the bus and be seated there. Now, most of those rear seats were empty. The Montgomery bus boycott ran for more than a year.

The U.S. Supreme Court ruled against allowing buses to be segregated. The Court said it was against the Constitution. "One day after the boycott ended," said Rosa Parks, "I rode a nonsegregated bus for the first time."[11]

Civil Rights Were Never Granted to All

"Civil" means relating to a community or its citizens. The rights to personal liberty and freedom are "civil rights." All citizens of a community should enjoy them. When the United States of America became a nation, its founders wrote a Constitution. This document is the main set of laws for the country. The opening or "preamble" to the Constitution talked about the "blessings of liberty." However, liberty has not always extended to everyone.

When the Constitution was adopted in 1787, most African Americans were slaves. They had no civil rights except those given by each state. In Southern states, the only right a slave had was life. His owner could not murder him without just cause.

After the Civil War was over in 1865, slaves were freed. The fifteenth amendment to the Constitution said men of every race and color now had the right to vote. However, state laws still restricted African Americans' right to vote and other rights.

A Long Struggle for Equal Rights

In 1955, Rosa Parks inspired African Americans to stand together. She helped them do what was right. However, the struggle for equality for American women and minorities did not begin then. This work started many years before Rosa Parks made her stand. It went back to America's birth as a nation.

Rights of Americans in the Constitution

Thirteen colonies lay along the east coast of America in 1775. They were ruled by Great Britain. King George III was the British monarch. British laws were made by a governing body called Parliament. British people sent representatives to this Parliament. The King did have power to influence the laws. He could also raise taxes or levy new ones. He could decide to go to war or make peace.

A Declaration

American colonists wanted to declare independence from Britain. Those who owned slaves did not want to free them. They feared that Britain would soon outlaw slavery. This is one of many reasons these colonists declared independence.

The Declaration of Independence was signed by a group of men from each colony. It was called "The unanimous Declaration of the thirteen united States of America." On July 4, 1776, it was adopted.

The Declaration stated that:
1. All men are created equal.
2. They all have the right to life, liberty, and the pursuit of happiness.
3. To get these rights, men need a government.
4. If a government denies these rights, men should abolish it and make a new one.

The declaration listed the "repeated injuries" that the King of Britain did to the colonists. They wrote a list of twenty-seven complaints. Most of them were about people's rights. The colonists wanted to have representatives decide on taxes. They wanted to have fair trials with honest judges. Each state must have its own charters and laws. The declaration also accused the king of exciting "the merciless Indian Savages" on the frontier to make war.[1] This referred to American Indians whom some colonists called "savages" because they thought the Indians were less advanced than them.

The war between Great Britain and the United States went on for seven years. A peace treaty was signed in Paris in 1783. Then, America needed a set of rules to run the government. They called these rules the Constitution of the United States. It was written to "secure a more perfect Union."

The Constitution was a good guide to running the government. Legislative powers were described for Congress, the main law-making body. Executive powers were given to the President. The judicial powers were laid out for the U.S. Supreme Court and the lower federal courts.

This painting of the signing of the Declaration of Independence was done by John Trumbull.

Individual Rights Must Be Assured

The authors of the Constitution noticed one thing missing from the document. There was no list of civil liberties for individuals.

Article Five of the Constitution said that two-thirds of Congress could vote to make an amendment. An amendment is something that is added to the original. Thomas Jefferson was a legislator and governor from Virginia. He had written the final draft of the Declaration of Independence. He wanted to see a "bill of rights" added to the Constitution.

James Madison, an author of the Constitution, thought a bill of rights was not needed. Madison wrote to Jefferson in October 1788. He said he favored the bill of rights, but he was afraid that it might "imply powers not meant to be included."[2] He meant these amendments had better be carefully written.

The bill of rights was proposed on September 25, 1789, but it did not pass until 1791. It included ten amendments:

1. The First Amendment assured people three major freedoms: free practice of religion, free speech, and a free press. It also assured people they could gather in peace and petition the government. In many other nations, there was a primary state religion, and people could not always practice the religion they wanted. A right to speak and publish freely, and even criticize the government, was also rare.

2. The Second Amendment gave the people the right to have a militia. This was a citizen force, not part of the national army. It also gave people the right to own personal weapons.

3. The Third Amendment allowed people the right to keep their homes private. They could not be forced to have soldiers stay in their homes.

4. The Fourth Amendment was about privacy. It said that people's homes could not be searched or things seized, unless the police had a warrant. No warrant could be given without good reason and probable cause.

5. The Fifth Amendment was about being held and tried for a crime. It said a person could not be tried for a capital crime (like murder) unless

a grand jury said so. It said a person could not be tried twice for the same crime. A person did not have to bear witness against himself. A person could never be put in prison, or his property taken, without due process of the law. Finally, no one's property could be taken for public uses without proper payment by the government.

6. The Sixth Amendment gave rights to a person accused of crimes: the right to a speedy and public trial; the right to a jury in the district where the crime was committed; to be told what he is accused of doing; to have all witnesses against him face him; and to have a lawyer for his defense.

7. The Seventh Amendment covered trials. In a common law suit where the value is more than twenty dollars, a man would be assured a trial by jury.

8. The Eighth Amendment gave people the right to reasonable bail and fines. It also said no one convicted could receive cruel and unusual punishment.

9. The Ninth Amendment said that certain rights are mentioned in the Constitution. They must not be used to deny other rights given to the people.

10. The Tenth Amendment said that powers not given to the federal government—or prohibited by the federal government to the states—would be given to the states. This amendment gave the states many rights. At the time it was written, it allowed any state to keep slavery if desired.[3]

The Constitution and the Bill of Rights did not clearly define two things. They did not say who is a citizen and they did not say who had the right to vote. It was assumed that citizens and voters were white adult men. Did a man need to own property? Did he have to be educated? These difficult issues were left out.

Over seventy years later, after the Civil War ended, the Fourteenth Amendment was added to the

Women and minorities did not get their civil liberties without a struggle.

Constitution. It said "All persons born or naturalized in the United States" were citizens. This included men and women of all races. It also said the right to vote must never be denied to any male inhabitant who was twenty-one years of age and a citizen. This included white and black men. Women were still not given this right.

Some Rights Were Hard to Get

Women and minorities did not get their civil liberties without a struggle. Theoretically, people had the right to free speech. Sometimes an African American spoke up to a white person. He might complain of some injustice. In some states, he or she could be hurt or jailed for this. Women spoke out and marched for the right to vote. Often they were fined or jailed for this. People had the right to own weapons. Their homes were private. African Americans sometimes had their homes invaded. In many cities, they could not own weapons. They had their homes searched without good cause.

When a black person was accused of a crime, he or she did not always have the same treatment as a white person. Sometimes an African American was hung by a mob without being arrested or given a fair trial. This kind of unfair execution was called a lynching. Other times black people were locked up without a lawyer or a fair trial. If there was a jury trial, the white jurors would often not listen to the African American's side. Women also had trouble getting a fair hearing.

State laws were hard to overturn. State laws kept blacks from voting, even when they had that constitutional right. State laws also kept other minorities from getting equal treatment. Throughout the nineteenth and twentieth centuries, the struggle continued.

African Americans Living in Slavery

Four million African Americans were slaves in the Southern states by 1860. Slaves, owners, and overseers worked near each other on plantations and farms. Slaves did all the backbreaking labor. The field slaves lived in cabins far from the owner; white overseers ran their lives. Household slaves stayed near their owner. They worked in the main house and gardens. They had to do their master's will at all times.

Groups of free African Americans lived in such southern cities as Baltimore, Maryland; Charleston, South Carolina; and New Orleans, Louisiana. A small number of free African Americans made a decent living. They worked as carpenters, barbers, craftspeople, and tradesmen. In Charleston, free blacks had to wear a metal tag that said "FREE." If they did not show the tag, they were thought to be slaves, and could be detained. Said historian Ira Berlin, "most were

In this engraving, enslaved African Americans pick cotton on a Southern plantation.

pushed into dismal poverty."[1] They were doing mostly the same labor as slaves.

Segregation the Rule for Free African Americans

More than half a million free African Americans lived in Northern states by 1860. Sometimes blacks and whites worked together at their jobs. A few white churches allowed African Americans to attend.

Otherwise, the races were separated, or "segregated." The racial codes that enforced segregation were not written down. White residents liked their neighborhoods, schools, and social clubs to stay all-white. Many white people felt more comfortable living separate from black people.

Discrimination against African Americans became a way of life. It differed from place to place. Only four states—Maine, Massachusetts, Vermont, and New Hampshire—let free African-American men vote. They were not allowed to serve on juries, though.

During the Revolutionary War, General George Washington had let free African-American men enlist in the army. He also let slaves fight beside their masters. Thousands of African-American soldiers were integrated in the Continental Army. After the war, segregation returned. Only New York and Louisiana allowed a black unit in their state militia.[2]

Abolitionists Try to Stop Slavery

Some white people believed slavery was wrong. They said slavery should be abolished. This meant slavery should be outlawed. These people were called abolitionists.

By 1840, hundreds of Northern towns and cities had antislavery societies. Abolitionists helped enslaved African Americans escape. They hid them as they traveled north. They helped them receive education. They tried to find jobs for them. The abolitionists' goal was to free all the slaves. The slave owners strongly resisted. They considered slaves their most valuable property.

In 1850, Congress passed the Fugitive Slave Law. Slave hunters searched for escaped African Americans. They captured the "runaway." They then took the slave back to his or her owner. Slave hunters received a large reward for these captures.

Often, escaped slaves had found jobs in the North.

They were settled in their communities. Slave hunters tore them away from jobs, family, and friends. The Fugitive Slave Law caused the abolitionists to work even harder against slavery.

Why We Fought a Civil War

There were several causes for the American Civil War in 1860. The conflict over slavery was surely a big reason. Historian William W. Freehling says that slavery was not the only reason. Eleven Southern states left the Union. Why did they do it? Slave-owning residents were willing to fight to keep their privileged life. Although 70 percent of Southern voters did *not* own slaves, they still felt the Southern states should be independent.

Power struggles between Northern and Southern politicians were one cause of the war. Illinois Congressman Abraham Lincoln was elected president in 1860. He wanted to end the slave states' control over the nation's territories and government.[3]

President Lincoln was a man of "moderate antislavery views," historian Don E. Fehrenbacher wrote.[4] Congressmen from the Northern states resented the Southerners' power. The North had the most seats in Congress. The North had financial means. Yet the South kept telling these legislators what to do.

Eleven states were committed to slave labor. They were Virginia, North and South Carolina, Tennessee, Georgia, Florida, Alabama, Louisiana, Mississippi, Arkansas, and Texas. They held their states' rights above the Union. When Lincoln became president, they feared he would not protect states' rights. They seceded, or left, the Union. Their secession caused the outbreak of civil war.

Union Victory Outlaws Slavery

The eleven seceded states formed the Confederate States of America. The Confederacy chose its own president and congress and formed an army. The capital was Richmond, Virginia.

The Union and the Confederacy fought bloody battles for four years. More than two hundred thousand African Americans fought for the Union. In 1863, President Abraham Lincoln signed the Emancipation Proclamation. This freed all the slaves in the Confederate states.

The Confederacy surrendered to the Union on April 9, 1865. Abraham Lincoln was then one month into his second term as president. On April 14, a stage actor named John Wilkes Booth assassinated him.

The Thirteenth Amendment to the Constitution was passed after Lincoln died in 1865. It abolished slavery throughout the United States. Four million African Americans were freed from their owners. They were on

During the Civil War, many African Americans who had once been slaves fought for the Union cause.

Harriet Beecher Stowe and Harriet Tubman

Harriet Beecher Stowe, born in 1811, was a well-educated white Northerner who lived in Cincinnati in the 1840s. She married scholar and professor Calvin Stowe and became a busy mother and author. Stowe's husband and brother were abolitionists. They helped slaves who had escaped. She heard the sad stories of slaves' lives from people who "conducted" slaves north on the "Underground Railroad." Stowe began to write. "I feel now that the time is come when even a woman or a child who can speak a word for freedom and humanity is bound to speak," Stowe said. "I hope every woman who can write will not be silent."[5]

Her novel *Uncle Tom's Cabin* was published in March 1852. It showed a harsh picture of slavery. The book inspired thousands of readers to push for abolition.

Harriet Tubman was born a slave in about 1820. She worked on a Maryland plantation. She endured hard labor. Author Sarah Bradford wrote about Tubman in 1869: "Powerful men often stood astonished to see this woman perform feats of strength from which they shrunk incapable."[6] Tubman longed for her freedom. She had no money or help. In her early twenties, she escaped. She walked nights and watched the North Star as her guide. By day, she hid from slave hunters. She made it across the Pennsylvania border. "I looked at my hands to see if I was [the] same person now [that] I was free," Bradford quoted her. "[There] was such a glory [over everything]. . . . I felt like I was in heaven."[7] Tubman decided to risk recapture. She went back nineteen times. More than 300 slaves got to freedom with Tubman's help.

Harriet Tubman risked her freedom about twenty times by sneaking into the South to help other African Americans get to the North and Canada.

their own. Most had little money or goods. Yet they felt the glory Harriet Tubman and other former slaves who had achieved freedom had described. Africans came to America, enslaved, in the early 1600s. Almost 250 years later, all African Americans were finally free.

African Americans Try to Make New Lives

The Civil War took six hundred twenty thousand lives. Thousands of wounded and disabled men went home. Families in the South barely survived. They were left with worthless money and damaged homes. Most African Americans were living in extreme poverty.

Congress wrote the Civil Rights Act of 1866. It gave black men the same rights as white citizens. They could make contracts and sue in court. They could buy, sell, or hold property. White men would be punished if they took away African-American men's rights.

Congress set up the Freedmen's Bureau offices. Workers there aided freed slaves. They tried to help settle families. Some freed families took over farms that whites left behind. They planted crops and formed small communities. Some freed men were trained as craftsmen and mechanics. They set up small businesses. A few moved west, to places like Kansas. They began new lives working as farmers or cowhands.

A Brief Chance at Forty Acres and a Mule

Many freed men wanted to start their own farms. They asked the government to give them this chance. They had no funds of their own. Islands off the coast of South Carolina and some property on the mainland Georgia and South Carolina were open for settlement, however.

Union General William Tecumseh Sherman issued Special Field Orders, Number 15. This set up a temporary plan granting each freed family forty acres of tillable land. A number of surplus army mules were also granted.[8]

When the Southern owners were pardoned by President Andrew Johnson, they fought to get the land back from the freed African-American families. The freedmen eventually lost their titles to these farms.

Most freed African Americans only knew how to farm. Without government aid, they had to become sharecroppers. They worked the land owned by whites. For this they received a modest wage. However, they had to buy their supplies from the plantation store. The plantation owner controlled the store's prices.

By the end of the year, most sharecroppers had no profit left. The store took all their wages. Often, they even owed money. They had to sign another contract to sharecrop. Some contracts lasted ten years. As historian Ronald Takaki wrote, such a sharecropper "found himself reduced to a 'lifetime slave.'"[9]

Trouble for Freed Slaves

General Ulysses S. Grant was elected president on November 3, 1868. African-American men cast seven hundred thousand votes for the winning ticket. White Southerners hated Grant. He was the man who led the

Frederick Douglass

Frederick Douglass was born in 1817 in Easton, Maryland, the son of a slave mother. He wrote in his autobiography that his father was a white man: "It was sometimes whispered that my master was my father."[10] He was later rented out to the Auld family in Baltimore. As a young boy, Frederick taught himself to read. Douglass escaped to the North in 1838. He further educated himself and became a popular speaker. Starting in 1847, he published his own newspaper, the *North Star*.

During the Civil War, Douglass wrote in the *North Star*: "We ask nothing at the hands of the American people but simple justice and an equal chance to live."[11] He helped enlist African Americans to fight for the Union. He insisted: "Slavery is not abolished until the black man has the ballot."[12]

Douglass lived to see the Fifteenth Amendment to the Constitution passed in 1870. It said no state could deny a *man* the right to vote, no matter what his race, color, or if he had been a slave. Douglass set high goals for his people. He wanted education and voter registration. He wanted ownership of property and equal rights. He died in 1895, soon after serving as U.S. Minister to Haiti.

Union Army during the Civil War. Federal troops had to keep the peace in the South when he won the presidential election.

Northern businessmen moved into Southern states. They wanted to make profits by rebuilding the South. Many Southern white men had survived the war. But they lost their pride. They took out their anger on freed African Americans.

Southern whites wanted to keep the freed men and women doing hard labor. They passed Black Codes. These local laws kept blacks from buying or renting except in special areas. They had to work long hours. They would be fined for vagrancy, or not being off the streets at night. They could be kept from buying a gun. Historian John Hope Franklin wrote, "The control of blacks by white employers was about as great as the control that slaveholders had exercised."[13]

Public Education and Civil Rights

The Freedmen's Bureau set up more than four thousand public schools for African-American children. Historian James M. McPherson noted: "Most of the good schools were located in the cities. . . . Schools in the countryside rarely functioned for more than three months a year."[14] In the 1870s, church groups from the North helped start colleges for African Americans. Fisk University, Howard University, Morehouse and Spelman colleges, and others, still operate today.

The Civil Rights Act of 1875 made discrimination by race against the law. By 1883, the Supreme Court ruled the 1875 law was unconstitutional. The court said that the Fourteenth Amendment (1868) gave Congress no power to legislate against discrimination by *individuals*. It ruled that private citizens could still discriminate against African Americans. The stage was set for decades of discrimination to come.

African Americans Are Kept Separate by State Laws

Three-quarters of African Americans lived in the South in 1890. Most were farmers. A million African Americans joined one farmers' union.[1] Other African Americans moved to cities located in Mississippi, Alabama, and Georgia. Men took jobs in factories. Women worked as maids.

Many whites wanted to keep the races apart. They used state laws to do this. In 1865, Mississippi had passed a law regulating train travel. African Americans could not ride in first-class passenger cars, which were set aside for white persons.[2]

Where *Jim Crow* Came From

"Jim Crow" laws were passed by some states. They kept blacks segregated. This nickname came from a character called "Jim Crow." He was part of minstrel shows. In these shows, white actors blackened their faces and hands. They wore foolish, tattered costumes. They joked and played the banjo. They made fun of being a slave. White actors never do minstrel shows today, because they are racist toward black people.

After the Civil War, "Jim Crow" became a slang term. White people used it to ridicule African-American men. Later, laws that segregated African Americans from whites were called Jim Crow laws.

Courts Rule on "Separate but Equal"

Advocates for equal rights wanted to test the Jim Crow laws. In Louisiana, an African American named Homer Plessy rode a train car. He sat in a first-class whites-only car. After he was arrested, he sued the railroad. In 1896, his case went to the U.S. Supreme Court. The case was called *Plessy v. Ferguson*.

The U.S. Supreme Court ruled that Plessy was not denied his rights. The train car may have been segregated. However, the car for African Americans was "equal" to the others. According to the court, riding in a separate but equal car did not stamp "the colored race with a badge of inferiority."[3]

Only one Supreme Court Justice, John Marshall Harlan, voted in favor of Plessy. He said, "Our Constitution is color-blind, and neither knows nor tolerates classes among citizens."[4] He said all citizens were equal before the law. The other justices voted against Plessy.

This court ruling upheld the Jim Crow laws. The "Colored Only" signs on buildings, restrooms, and train cars remained.

Ida B. Wells-Barnett

Ida B. Wells was born in Mississippi in 1862 to a slave family. After her family was freed, Wells took care of her five brothers and sisters when she was sixteen. In 1884, Wells had a bitter experience with a Jim Crow law. A train conductor told her to ride in the second-class "smoker" car. Wells had a first-class ticket. She refused to move. The conductor forced her off the train. Wells sued the railroad. She lost her case but not her courage. Ida B. Wells became a journalist. She worked with the National Afro-American League. This was an early group that promoted civil rights. Wells told the League's president, "Agitate and act until *something* is done."[5]

In 1893, the World's Columbian Exposition opened in Chicago. African Americans at the fair would be segregated. There, she met attorney-editor F. L. Barnett. They published a book to explain why they were boycotting the fair.

Wells and Barnett married and raised four children. Wells-Barnett protested against lynching. *Lynching* meant a mob hanging a person before they had a trial or conviction by law. She begged people to speak out against it. Wells-Barnett also worked for women's rights. She started African-American women's clubs. She was a founder of the National Association for the Advancement of Colored People (NAACP).

African Americans Want Equality from Government

In 1912, African Americans were hopeful about the new president, Woodrow Wilson. He ran against two former presidents, William Howard Taft and Theodore Roosevelt. President Roosevelt had not supported equality. In 1906, men in an African-American Infantry unit serving in Brownsville, Texas were dishonorably discharged. Rumors circulated that several soldiers were involved in a murder. These soldiers deserved a fair trial, but no trial was held. Roosevelt let their discharge stand.

When President Wilson made his inaugural speech in March 1913, he promised to remember all the people. However, he failed to stand up for African Americans. Wilson allowed segregation practices in federal government offices and agencies to continue.

World War I Explodes

World War I began in Europe in the summer of 1914. Woodrow Wilson tried to keep America out of this war. Then, in early 1917, German submarines destroyed five U.S. merchant ships. Wilson asked Congress to declare war against Germany.

America needed soldiers. African Americans had proudly served in the military since the American Revolution. They eagerly joined up in 1917. Historian Philip Klinkner states that almost four hundred thousand African-American soldiers served in Europe. But, he noted, "World War I led to no great advance for black rights."[6]

African Americans were kept in their own units. These units had white commanding officers. The NAACP complained. If units had to be segregated, they should have African-American officers. The army agreed. More than six hundred black officers trained and commissioned in 1917.[7] African-American soldiers worked mostly in support services. However, over forty thousand did serve in combat. The French government honored these soldiers.

When African-American soldiers came home after the war, they wanted respect as veterans. But racism still existed in jobs and housing. African-American leader W. E. B. Du Bois wrote in *Crisis* magazine about the returning soldiers. He said: "We return fighting! Make way for Democracy! We saved it in France . . . and we will save it in the United States of America, or know the reason why."[8] The respect Du Bois wanted did not happen. Between 1919 and 1922, at least 239 African Americans were lynched. Ten black soldiers, still wearing their uniforms, were among them.[9]

Some Urban Whites Resent Black Communities

Many African Americans quit farming. They moved to cities, and trouble started. African-American workers took the lower-level jobs. Whites thought they were stealing their work. Anger simmered into violence. Whites fought, believing the police would be on their side.

Whites fought blacks in East St. Louis, Missouri, and Houston, Texas, in the summer of 1917. In 1918, riots started in Philadelphia, Pennsylvania, and in Nashville, Tennessee. In 1919, seven more cities had racial violence. Chicago's conflicts saw 38 dead, 23 black and 15 white, and 291 wounded.[10]

One of the worst riots tore apart Tulsa, Oklahoma,

William Edward Burghardt (W. E. B.) Du Bois was born in 1868 in Great Barrington, Massachusetts. Du Bois earned three degrees. One was a doctorate from Harvard. His goal was to see African Americans gain racial pride. He was a founder and director of publicity for the NAACP. Later he edited their journal, *Crisis*. Du Bois said in 1906: "We want full manhood suffrage and we want it now. We want discrimination in public accommodations to cease. . . . we want the Constitution of the country enforced. . . . we will be treated as men!"[11]

Du Bois was a leader in the Pan-African Congress. This group united blacks from around the world. Du Bois urged education and pride for the African-American family. He preached that "people may ride in the backs of streetcars and the smoker end of trains, and still be . . . honest high-minded souls."[12]

in 1921. Thousands of national guardsmen tried to stop it. It is estimated that over three hundred people were killed and about twelve hundred homes destroyed.[13]

Small Victories During Hard Times

In 1929, the world was experiencing an economic depression. In America, many banks and companies closed. Urban African Americans had a tough time. Their unemployment number was almost twice as high as the number of white people with no job. People with college degrees took jobs as laborers and maids. Black men lost their low-level jobs to whites. A third of urban African-American families needed public aid for food.

In the 1930s, African-American leaders asked people to avoid businesses that would not hire blacks.[14] They called this "Don't Buy Where You Can't Work." This boycott to fight racism in hiring spread from the Midwest to New York City.

Racial hatred grew during these hard times. In 1930, lynchings were still common. Two African Americans, ages eighteen and nineteen, were hung in Marion, Indiana. The young men were accused of murder. They had no trial. Photos show a white crowd beneath the hanging corpses. They are having a "lynching party"[15]

African-American Groups are Founded

The NAACP (founded in 1909) and the National Urban League (organized in 1911) had long fought for equal rights. These groups had both black and white members. The NAACP worked through the courts for justice.

Wallace D. Fard was a Detroit salesman. In 1930, he began the Nation of Islam (NOI). The NOI was both religious and political. Fard taught the religion of Islam for African Americans. People called it the Black Muslim Movement. Historian Eric Lincoln wrote about the NOI. He said, "they are reaching for the support of the entire Negro lower class."[16] The NOI continued later under Elijah Mohammed and Malcolm X.

The Fight for Fairness in Employment

In 1932, Franklin D. Roosevelt was elected President. At this time, America faced severe economic problems. Roosevelt made government loans to many African-American farmers. Men of all races got jobs in the Works Progress Administration (WPA), part of the New Deal. They built construction projects. African Americans could join trade unions, but still many had no job.

In 1940, the Nazi government of Germany and its allies were at war in Europe. Japan was Germany's ally. Japan bombed America's bases at Pearl Harbor, Hawaii, in 1941. Roosevelt asked Congress to declare war on Japan. In 1941, A. Philip Randolph was president of a large union of black railroad workers. He

James Farmer

Some University of Chicago students wanted to protest for equal rights. They would use only peaceful means. They named their group the Congress of Racial Equality (CORE). James Farmer was one of its first leaders. He was an African-American student from the South. Farmer knew that public places and buses were still segregated. CORE would protest by "sit-ins" and picketing. "My ambition was to wage war on racism," Farmer said. But CORE would never fight back with violence.[17]

Farmer wanted equal rights for all. CORE members became "freedom riders." African-American members sat in places marked "For Whites Only." Often they were ridiculed and beaten. Farmer did not give up. He became CORE's first National Director in 1953.

protested unfairness in hiring. Randolph asked President Roosevelt not to give defense contracts to factories if they refused to hire African-American workers. Randolph said: "Our nearer goals include the abolition of discrimination, segregation, and jim-crow in the Government, the Army, Navy, Air Corps, U.S. Marine. . . . We want the full works of citizenship with no reservations."[18] Randolph said he could get seventy-five thousand African Americans to march with him. They would picket the White House.

To avoid this, President Roosevelt issued Executive Order 8802. It said a defense company must hire fairly. Otherwise, it will lose its government contract. Roosevelt formed the Fair Employment Practice Committee (FEPC). This committee enforced the Executive Order.

African-American leaders also asked Roosevelt to integrate the military. They did not want blacks-only units. President Roosevelt disagreed, so African Americans fought World War II in segregated units. Again, they were put mostly in service jobs. For many African-American men, the military was still a good job. For defending their country, they got more pay and respect than before.

When Roosevelt died on April 12, 1945, Vice President Harry S. Truman became president. He appointed a Committee on Civil Rights, which produced a report called "To Secure These Rights." It recommended government action "to end immediately all discrimination and segregation . . . [in] the Armed Services."[19]

These three African-American soldiers are training to operate a communications radio at Fort Benning, Georgia, in 1941 before they leave America to fight in World War II.

Truman and members of his Democratic Party put civil rights in their 1948 party platform. Truman was reelected. He carried out his party's promise. He said he believed most Americans "understand that the blind prejudices of past generations cannot continue in a free republic."[20] As commander in chief, Truman signed Executive Order 9981 in July 1948. It ended racial segregation in the armed forces.

Segregated Schools Are *Not* Equal

African Americans were told their schools were separate but equal. They knew this was not true. The schools for their children were separate. But they were not equal.

Surveys of schools in the South were done in the 1920s. One survey said eight times more money was spent on white students than on blacks. In South Carolina, class size in black schools was twice as big as in schools for whites. In Sparta, Georgia, white teachers were paid an average of $7,550 a year in the 1920s. The salary paid to black teachers averaged $702. A survey said "half of the schools for the colored children are taught in churches, lodge halls, and dwellings."[1] Pupils had few books. Schools had not gotten much better.

Most white parents wanted separate schools. The *Plessy vs. Ferguson* ruling allowed this. African-American parents wanted their children to go to the better schools. These were reserved for whites only.

The Brown sisters sit in their segregated classroom. In the lower right corner is Linda Brown, the girl to the left of the lefthand door is Terry Lynn Brown.

The Brown Family Makes History

The Browns lived in Topeka, Kansas, in 1951. Linda Brown went to third grade. Terry Brown went to kindergarten. These African-American girls lived near a white public school. They were forced to take a long dangerous walk to their bus stop. Then they had to ride a bus. Finally they got to their African-American school far from home.

Their father, Reverend Oliver Brown, was angry about this. He asked the Kansas NAACP to represent his family. Reverend Brown sued the school board. He wanted to send his girls to the nearby white public school.

Thurgood Marshall

Thurgood Marshall was born in 1908 in Baltimore. He earned his law degree from Howard University in Washington, D.C. Eventually, he became the NAACP's chief lawyer and worked on civil rights cases including *Brown* v. *Board of Education*. Because he wanted equal education for all, racists threatened his life. In 1950, Marshall led a team that won two U.S. Supreme Court rulings. Because of his efforts African Americans could attend all-white graduate schools. Marshall's team ended the "separate but equal" law.[2] In 1967, he became the first African American to serve on the Supreme Court.

The case was called *Oliver Brown et. al.* v. *Board of Education of Topeka*. The case went through the courts. In the Supreme Court, all the justices ruled in favor of Oliver Brown. This decision overruled *Plessy* v. *Ferguson*. On May 17, 1954, Chief Justice Earl Warren said: "We conclude . . . that in the field of public education the doctrine of 'separate but equal' has no place."[3] The district courts would enforce integration for their public schools.

Integrating Schools Causes Resistance

In both the North and South, white people were stunned at the *Brown* Supreme Court ruling. Some citizens slowly accepted the idea. Some white families moved to all-white towns. Some states funded private schools for white pupils.

In September 1957, the governor of Arkansas was Orval Faubus. He refused to obey the court. He kept Arkansas schools segregated. The NAACP found nine brave African-American students. These nine agreed to test the law. They enrolled in Central High of Little Rock. Students and townspeople jeered at them. Faubus sent in the Arkansas National Guard. These soldiers stopped the "Little Rock Nine" from attending school.

President Dwight D. Eisenhower went on national television. He said that America was losing its good image with other nations. America set high standards of conduct. Now we violated those standards.[4] Eisenhower sent in Federal troops. They helped the Little Rock Nine to attend school.

The Little Rock Nine made it to their classes. Ernest Green graduated in 1958. Governor Faubus closed Little Rock's public schools during 1959. Private schools were started for white students. Central High reopened in 1960. Jefferson Thomas and Carlotta Walls Lanier got their degrees. The other six black students left. They finished at other high schools. All nine got good jobs.

President Eisenhower signed the 1957 Civil Rights Act. The U.S. Commission on Civil Rights was established. The act helped minorities register to vote.

Freedom Riders Integrate the South

More marches and sit-ins were organized. Civil rights groups wanted to force integration in the South. Anger and fear were deeply rooted in white people. "Freedom Marchers" were cursed and assaulted. African Americans and their supporters would have to march many miles before segregation was ended.

The NAACP and CORE were joined by the Southern Christian Leadership Conference (SCLC) in 1957. College students formed the Student Nonviolent Coordinating Committee (SNCC) in 1960. This group used peaceful protest, declaring "Nonviolence . . . seeks a social order of justice permeated by love."[5]

SNCC and CORE worked together on a Freedom Ride. James Peck was a white Northerner with CORE. He had participated in a Freedom Ride in 1947. He joined the group of SNCC riders in May 1961. They would peacefully integrate buses and waiting rooms.

Peck and his group rode to Anniston, Alabama. A mob attacked their bus. They broke windows and threw in a firebomb. They held the bus doors closed. Peck and the others barely escaped the fire.

Peck rode on to Birmingham, Alabama. Another mob waited. Peck and the riders were beaten with iron bars. "Within seconds, I was unconscious on the ground," he recalled.[6] Peck's wounds needed fifty-three stitches. Peck and the riders went on to Montgomery. There a mob of more than a thousand whites attacked them. Peck still rode on.

Through the summer of 1961, blacks and whites in civil rights groups protested for justice. Many were arrested. The more educated members ran classes for African Americans. These were called Freedom Schools. Volunteers taught basic reading skills and how to register to vote.

Protestors are knocked down by water from powerful fire hoses in Birmingham, Alabama, on July 15, 1963.

During 1963 in Birmingham, Alabama, Reverend Martin Luther King, Jr., led a march for integration. Almost twenty-five thousand men, women, and children joined him. The Public Safety Commissioner wanted the march to stop. He ordered police dogs and fire hoses to be used against the demonstrators. He jailed many leaders. News reports showed the racial division in America.

Kennedy Prepares a Civil Rights Act

President John F. Kennedy knew a federal law was needed to assure civil rights. This law would help stop racial conflict. However, Kennedy was murdered on

Martin Luther King, Jr.

Born in Atlanta in 1929, Martin Luther King, Jr., was a fine student. He earned a Ph.D. in religious studies. As a Baptist minister and father of four, he preached justice and love. He said: "We have waited . . . for our constitutional and God-given rights . . . we still creep at horse-and-buggy pace toward the gaining of a cup of coffee at a lunch counter."[7] His goal was to see equal rights for all.

Dr. King inspired thousands. On August 28, 1963, he led a March for Jobs and Freedom in Washington, D.C. More than two hundred thousand marchers joined him at the Lincoln Memorial there. He said all people needed justice. The right to life, liberty, and the pursuit of happiness belonged to everyone. "I have a dream," he said, "that one day on the red hills of Georgia, sons of former slaves and sons of former slave-owners will be able to sit down together at the table of brotherhood."[8]

On December 10, 1964, Dr. King accepted the Nobel Peace Prize. He was honored for his nonviolent protests for equal rights. He continued to fight for world peace. On April 4, 1968, he was murdered in Memphis, Tennessee.

Martin Luther King, Jr., waves to the crowd in Washington, D.C., during the August 28, 1963 march on Washington.

November 22, 1963. The law he asked for was the Civil Rights Act. On July 2, 1964, it became law.

The act "guaranteed equal political, social, and economic *rights* to all Americans." These rights were given to people of every race, color, religion, or national origin.[9] President Lyndon B. Johnson signed it.

Also in 1964, the Twenty-fourth Amendment to the Constitution was passed. It said that no one needed to pay money (called a "poll tax") in order to vote. This tax had been hard for poor people, especially black voters who were denied the better jobs.

President Johnson spoke to Congress on March 15, 1965. This date was almost one hundred years after the Civil War ended. He spoke of "the long denial of equal rights of millions of Americans. But there is cause for hope and faith in our democracy in what is happening here tonight."[10]

President Johnson signed the Voting Rights Act on August 6, 1965. No one would have to pass a voter reading test again. Only a decade had gone by since African-American children were allowed to go to integrated schools. Their parents often did not have strong reading skills because of poor schooling for blacks. So many black voters found it hard to pass the reading test, and could not vote. This barrier was now gone.

Urban Rioting Breaks Out

In 1967, riots erupted in many large cities. Detroit; Newark, New Jersey; New York; Cleveland, Ohio; Washington, D.C.; Chicago; and Atlanta all had trouble.

In Detroit alone, forty-three people died. More than five thousand were left homeless. Some riots were blamed on heat and poverty. Some people felt police actions caused riots. Some riots started as racial gang fights.

A national commission studied the problems. Illinois Governor Otto Kerner was chairman. Kerner said that our nation was becoming two societies. One was white, and one was black. "Discrimination and segregation . . . now threaten the future of every American," said Kerner.[11]

Urban African Americans Try for a Better Life

Large groups of African Americans living in cities tried to improve their jobs and housing. The struggle was hard. They did make an impact by voting. Many African-American candidates were elected. The mayors of Cleveland, Los Angeles, Atlanta, and Detroit were African Americans. Shirley Chisholm of New York was the first African-American woman in Congress. In 1972, she ran for President.

Integration in public schools was now the law. One way to balance the races was to bus pupils. Many African-American children were bused to schools with more white children. Some white families' response was to move. Many African-American parents were not comfortable with busing, either.

The number of African-American students in college soared. These black college graduates tried to land good jobs. However, they were often turned away because of their race.

Affirmative Action and Minorities

President John F. Kennedy was the first to use the term "Affirmative Action." He wrote about it in an order in 1961. Certain companies were owned and run by members of minority races. They had been denied contracts because of prejudice. Under Kennedy's affirmative action, these companies were now to be favored and given special preference. Title VII became part of the Civil Rights Act of 1964. It made affirmative action a law.

Historian Hugh Davis Graham said, "under affirmative action the rights of American citizens were not everywhere the same."[12] This policy made up for past bias against minorities.

President Richard M. Nixon revived the timetable to achieve Title VII in 1969. He said he believed "a good job is as basic and important a civil right as a good education."[13] President James Earl "Jimmy" Carter in 1977 also favored federal contracts for people of minority races. Hispanics, Native Americans, and Asians, as well as African Americans and women, were all classed as minorities.

Was Affirmative Action a Fair Policy?

In the 1980s, both white people and minorities started to wonder if affirmative action was fair. For example, the Detroit Symphony Orchestra put people who wanted to audition behind a screen. That way the judges hired each new player "blind," without knowing their race or gender. An African-American musician in 1984 told the Michigan legislature that this was wrong. The judges should "encourage the identification and selection of qualified black applicants."[14] The legislature said the auditions must "assure the hiring of [minority] musicians."[15]

Although a black musician was hired next, no one was happy at the symphony. Some felt standards were now lower. The new African-American bass player wanted to be hired strictly for his talent. He felt he would have to prove himself every day to the other musicians. Affirmative action did not always work.

In 1991, arguments over this policy created another Civil Rights Act. It was to protect civil rights rulings and affirmative action programs. Some people thought it would lead to "hiring quotas." This meant that companies would *have* to hire a certain number of minority people. President George H. W. Bush, who signed this Civil Rights Act, said it would *not* lead to quotas. It would help truly qualified people of all races and genders get hired.[16]

During this period, affirmative action did call attention to the largest group in America who were not treated equally. This group was American women. They were also asking for equal rights in hiring. Their fight for their rights began in the early nineteenth century. By the end of the twentieth century, women's struggle continued.

Women Are Not Treated Equally

During the 1840s, some American women began to question their lack of rights. As soon as they married, they lost rights to their property and money. By 1848, New York State did pass a Married Woman's Property Act. However, most states had no such laws.

Women wanted higher education. Most were working in the home or on the farm. Some women held jobs as teachers and writers. They could not be trained for other fields. Also, women had no representation. They had not been given suffrage. "Suffrage" means the right to vote in a political election.

Lucretia Mott and Elizabeth Cady Stanton were forward-thinking women. They decided to call a meeting. They would discuss equal rights for women. Women needed rights to education, property, and the vote. In Seneca Falls, New York, in July 1848, many others gathered with Mott and Stanton. They quoted the Declaration of Independence: "We hold these truths to be self-evident: that all *men are created equal*." They said that this meant both men *and* women.

Women Abolitionists Become Suffragists

Most of the early women's rights workers wanted to abolish slavery. At the Seneca Falls meeting, Cady Stanton spoke. She was the daughter of a diplomat and the wife of a politician. When the slaves were freed, said Cady Stanton, African-American men would be given the vote. Should not this be *women's* chance to have it also?

Some of the three hundred persons attending thought Cady Stanton was too extreme. Historian Lois Banner later stated that Cady Stanton also favored the controversial ideas of divorce reform and birth control.[1] A woman had a hard time suing for divorce in 1848. Birth control information was almost impossible to get.

Lucretia Mott was one of the first leaders of the women's suffrage movement.

One of the few males at Seneca Falls was ex-slave Frederick Douglass. He spoke strongly for the vote for all. He persuaded the women to make suffrage their cause.

During the 1850s, Mott and Cady Stanton held meetings for women's rights. They pushed for

Elizabeth Cady Stanton (left) and Susan B. Anthony

their reforms. Julia Ward Howe and Lucy Stone from Boston started a New England association for women's rights.

Women are Passed Over

The Fifteenth Amendment to the Constitution passed in 1870. It did not grant women the right to vote. Voting could not be denied because of race, color, or previous enslavement. It did not mention gender or sex.

In 1870, another women's suffrage meeting was held in New York. It was over twenty years since women met at Seneca Falls, New York. Had women progressed? Mrs. Paulina Wright Davis made a report.

Davis stated that women were still "slaves of prejudice . . . fashion and petty ambitions."[2] She wanted women to be responsible for their own lives. Davis also blamed men. She said they looked down on half of the human race.

Matilda Gage spoke on women's progress. In 1850 only Antioch and Oberlin colleges admitted women. By 1870, many colleges admitted women. Gage listed several public colleges in the Midwest, as well as Cornell University in Ithaca, New York. Private women's colleges were opening. "There are seven medical colleges wholly for women . . . and a few others which admit women with men," said Gage.[3] Gage stated that more than twenty women were studying theology in America at that time. About one hundred women studied to be lawyers. Women were also working as "stenographers, engravers,

Lucy Stone, born in 1818 in Massachusetts, worked her way through Oberlin College. She was the first woman from Massachusetts to earn a bachelor's degree. She spoke for abolition and women's rights. Later, she became an editor. She said: "I expect to plead not for the slave only, but for suffering humanity everywhere. Especially do I mean to labor for the elevation of my sex."[4] In 1855, Stone married businessman Henry Blackwell. He also favored equal rights. Stone's sister-in-law Elizabeth Blackwell was America's first woman doctor. Another in-law, Antoinette Brown, was America's first female ordained minister. This amazing family backed Stone's beliefs.

Stone founded the American Woman Suffrage Association (AWSA) in 1869. She told her daughter Alice Stone Blackwell that women could be happy at home with their families. All they needed was "pecuniary [financial] freedom, personal freedom, and the right to vote."[5]

The Civil War ended in 1865. Susan B. Anthony and Elizabeth Cady Stanton appealed to Congress. They demanded women's suffrage. Their National Woman Suffrage Association (NWSA) was founded in 1869. Their goal was to amend the Constitution. Lucy Stone and the AWSA worked on the state and local level. They wanted each state to recognize women's suffrage.[6] These two groups began the legal battle for women's equal rights.

printers, photographers, engineers, druggists, dentists, merchants, clerks, book-keepers, . . . real estate and insurance agents."[7]

Gage listed a dozen other professions. She stated there was a still a double standard in law and marriage. Men had certain rights, and women did not.

Victoria Woodhull

Victoria Claflin, born in 1838, came from a terrible background. Her parents were thieves. Victoria worked for her abusive father as a child preacher and spiritualist. Victoria married Dr. Canning Woodhull. He was an older doctor who drank too much. She was only fifteen. She said: "My marriage was an escape."[8]

Woodhull and her sister became self-educated stockbrokers. Woodhull was determined to see women get equal rights. In 1870, she had a memorial read to Congress. No woman had ever done this. The memorial stated that women were citizens. It quoted the Fourteenth Amendment: "No state shall make or enforce any law which shall abridge [reduce] the privileges . . . of citizens." Therefore, women have the constitutional right to vote.[9] Woodhull begged women: "Rise and declare . . . yourself free. Women are entirely unaware of their power."[10]

Women suffragists were pleased at Woodhull's logic. Congressmen did not agree. Woodhull offered to run for President. Her bold ideas about women's rights opened many minds.

Victoria Woodhull spoke to the judiciary committee of the House of Representatives on January 11, 1871, on the subject of a woman's right to vote.

Women Fight for Jobs and Salaries

By 1890, many white women worked in Northern factories and mills. Their jobs were hard and repetitious. Their wages were lower than the wage for a man. Their attempts to strike for fair wages failed. In Atlanta and Columbus, Georgia, black washerwomen held out for higher wages in 1891. They formed a union and got better conditions.

Gaining Women's Suffrage State by State

Jessie Haver heard tales of her mother. Mrs. Haver toured her Colorado valley in her wagon. She made speeches for suffrage. "This wasn't something a good little housewife . . . in those days was supposed to do," said Jessie.[11] Her mother was inspired by Susan B. Anthony. Tiny, courageous Anthony rode donkeys through the mountains. She spoke to Colorado miners in their saloons. Colorado women won suffrage in 1893.

In three more Western states, women won the right to vote. They were Wyoming (1890), Utah (1895), and Idaho (1896). It seemed suffrage was about to happen nationwide.

Why the Movement Slowed Down

Alice Stone Blackwell was Lucy Stone's daughter. Harriot Stanton Blatch was Elizabeth Cady Stanton's daughter. These young women got their mothers' groups together. The National Woman Suffrage Association merged with the American Woman

Suffrage Association. Their new group was named the National American Woman Suffrage Association (NAWSA). Carrie Chapman Catt, another younger member, became president.

NAWSA campaigned for the vote in thirty-three states. The group influenced seventeen states to vote on women's suffrage. But they won only *two* victories. The NAWSA leadership was weakened. Older leaders died during this period. Suffrage campaigns in the East were poorly organized. Southern women did not push for suffrage. Many felt voting was best left to men. They thought women's suffrage was a Northern notion.

Harriot Stanton Blatch returned in 1909 from London. British women were still fighting for full suffrage. In 1869 only unmarried British women were given the vote in local elections. The British used public speeches and parades to spread their message.

Blatch founded the Women's Political Union in New York. This group organized the first American women's suffrage parade. They marched in New York in 1910.

Suffragists Disagree on Methods

The National American Woman Suffrage Association (NAWSA) ran into problems. Some members believed that suffrage must come state by state. They thought Congress was too divided to pass a national amendment. Some believed African-American women were not their equals. They did not want suffrage for them. Other militant members felt a national amendment was possible. These differences caused friction.

Women suffragists picket in front of the White House in February 1917.

Picketing and Parades Keep Suffrage Alive

President Woodrow Wilson avoided the issue of a suffrage amendment. His policy was to let each state decide. Alice Paul had already led a large protest march at his 1913 inauguration. By the end of 1917, President Wilson had to notice the women's protests. They kept holding them in front of his White House windows.

Historians say that at least five hundred women were arrested for unlawful picketing. Serious jail sentences were given to 168 women.[12] The National Women's Party kept up the pressure. A photo showed college students picketing the White House in 1917. They wore sashes identifying their schools. These women held a banner that asked: "Mr. President What Will You Do For Woman Suffrage."[13]

Women Fight for the Right to Vote

Woodrow Wilson had tried to stop the march for women's suffrage. Finally, he gave in and supported the vote for women. Representatives brought the suffrage amendment to Congress in 1918.

The Nineteenth Amendment to the Constitution was passed by Congress in January 1919. By 1920, it had been ratified by the thirty-six states needed. No one could any longer be denied the vote because of gender. Women across the land celebrated.

Laws Deny Women Other Equal Rights

However, women knew they still lacked full equal rights. They could not serve on juries. They did not receive equal pay for equal work. They could not control their property in most states. Many felt an Equal Rights Amendment (ERA) was needed. In 1929, Representative Daniel Anthony proposed this amendment to Congress in the 1930s. Daniel was the nephew of Susan B. Anthony. However Congress failed to approve this amendment.

In the 1930s, the economy was very depressed.

Poor women had to work to support their families. Before the stock market crashed in 1929, middle-class women were going to college. They landed jobs as clerks, secretaries, and salespeople. Some even held management positions. Then many businesses failed. Owners felt every job left should go to a man. Women were fired. Most schools would not hire married women to teach.

World War II Offers Women New Jobs

World War II changed the job picture for women. In 1941, men were called into the armed services. Women gladly took their factory jobs. One million women were hired by the government to handle war-related jobs. Women soon made up 40 percent of the workers in aircraft plants.[1] A government survey states that by 1944, the number of women employed had risen by 48 percent. Over 3 million women joined trade unions.[2]

Women had not been allowed to join the military before. Several groups of nurses had volunteered to serve in France during World War I. Now the armed forces badly needed people.

Almost four hundred thousand women joined the military during World War II.[3] They freed male soldiers to fight in battle. Women did everything else. They nursed in the Army and Navy Nurse Corps. They did jobs for the Army Air Force and the Women's Army Auxiliary Corp (WAAC). At sea, women joined the Navy's Women Accepted for Volunteer Emergency Service (WAVES). The Marine Corps had its Women's

Women work on the propeller of a C-47 Douglas cargo transport plane in Long Beach, California, during World War II.

Reserve. Women sailed with the Coast Guard. Women Airforce Service Pilots (WASPs) flew cargo and transported planes to military bases.

At first, General Dwight Eisenhower did not want women in the military. He wondered how would they hold up under pressure. However, soon he changed his mind. Women became his best-disciplined soldiers. Women served everywhere except on battle lines. They braved all dangers. The enemy captured eighty-eight women. Enemy fire killed 432 women.[4] Many were awarded medals.

The Army Nurse Corps trained about twenty-five hundred African-American women. They were only allowed to care for black troops in black wards.[5] These nurses served in Africa, England, Burma, and the Pacific region.

At home, women volunteered long hours. They worked for the American Red Cross, the United Service Organization (USO), and the Civil Air Patrol.

The ERA Surfaces After the War

The Equal Rights Amendment (ERA) had been "buried" in Congress. Finally, in 1946, it received a hearing. The wording was a little different from the first one Alice Paul wrote in 1921. The ERA now said: "Equality of rights under the law shall not be denied or abridged by the United States or by any state on account of sex."[6]

Congress understood the role of women's work for the war. This time thirty-five Senators voted in favor.

However, thirty-eight voted no. The ERA again failed to pass.

The war had ended in September 1945. Veterans returned to look for work. There were no labor laws to protect women's jobs. Many women were glad to become housewives again. Others wanted and needed their jobs. Most female defense workers were fired as war veterans took their jobs.

Should Women Work Full-Time?

After the war, the nation enjoyed a time of growth. Business picked up. By the end of the 1940s, new jobs were opening for women. Should they take them? Many needed these jobs. Some were single, widowed, or divorced. Some had husbands earning a low wage.

Wives were unsure about leaving home to work. Would their children suffer? Few could find good child care. Family planning was a big issue. Employers feared women would keep getting pregnant and not be steady workers. Employment caused many problems for women to solve.

Women like Margaret Sanger and Mary Dennett had been working since 1914 on family planning. Sanger said it was a woman's right to decide when or whether to have a child; she said every child should be wanted and loved.[7]

The Comstock Act of 1873 said no one could distribute information about sex and reproduction. Sanger and Dennett practiced "civil disobedience," and passed out flyers about sex. This meant they broke the law on purpose. They did so because they felt the law needed to be reformed. Both women served time in jail. Slowly, the laws changed. People got information on birth control. Sanger became President of the Planned Parenthood Federation of America in the 1950s.

Women Are Torn Between Home and Job

More jobs were opening for women. Wars had killed or disabled many men. There were high death rates for soldiers in World War II (1941–1945) and the Korean War (1950–1953). The American Battle Monuments Commission lists 405,399 dead for World War II and

If women got jobs, they were not promoted as fast as men. They did not get the same pay or raises as men.

54,246 dead for the Korean War.[8] Thousands of widows were left in charge of households. They needed good jobs to pay the bills.

In the mid-1950s, the economy was growing. Americans enjoyed prosperity. Middle- and upper-class white families were thriving. Women who married in the 1950s had a common goal. They would be good homemakers, mothers, and community volunteers. For many women, achieving this goal made them happy.

Other women had different issues. Single women, minorities, or women with low-income husbands, still

Bella (Savitsky) Abzug

Bella Savitsky wanted a career and a family. Born in 1920, she was president of the Student Government at Hunter College of New York and won a scholarship to Columbia University Law School. She wed Martin Abzug, a business-man and stockbroker, who encouraged her to practice law.

Abzug took unpopular cases. She helped people who were discriminated against. In Mississippi, an African American named Willie McGee was arrested for raping a white woman. No white attorneys would take his appeal. Even though she was expecting a child in 1951, Abzug put her safety aside. She defended McGee. She argued his appeal for six hours straight. Although she lost, Abzug continued to fight for justice.

Abzug raised two children. At age fifty, she was elected to Congress. Her slogan was: "This woman's place is in the House—the House of Representatives!"[9] She served the people of New York for three terms. Abzug was a founder of the National Women's Political Caucus in 1971. This group supported women running for office. She wrote bills for help with child care and family planning. In the 1970s, she chaired the National Advisory Commission for Women.

Bella Abzug joins a demonstration in order to save a day care center.

needed jobs. Middle-class white women had a choice. Some chose to pursue a career.

Companies often did not hire women at the same rate as men. If women got jobs, they were not promoted as fast as men. They did not get the same pay or raises as men.

Divorce Laws Need Correcting

The divorce rate was rising. State divorce laws hurt women. For example, New York divorce laws were unfair to poor women. Rich women could go to Mexico or to a state like Nevada for an easy divorce. Poor women who could not leave had a difficult struggle. Grounds for divorce were hard to prove. Poor women could not afford good lawyers. These women often did not end up with a fair settlement.

Janet Hill Gordon and other New York legislators fought for reform. In 1966, the Divorce Reform Law was passed.[10] Grounds for divorce were broader. They now included physical or mental cruelty to wives. The law added "no-fault" grounds based on separation. Divorce became easier for poor wives to get.

Women Try to Expand Their Roles

What equal rights were women missing? Women in the workplace knew the answer. Employers did not have to give women equal treatment. Many jobs were still not open to females. On the job, women faced discrimination.

Plus, they did not feel connected to women who worked at home. There was little sense of sisterhood.

By the end of the 1950s, women demanded equal pay for equal work. Many helped elect John F. Kennedy president in 1960. They believed he would get the Equal Rights Amendment passed. Women were disappointed when President Kennedy did not push for the ERA.

Betty Goldstein Friedan had both a family and dreams of a career. She graduated from Smith College in 1942. She married an advertising executive. They had three children. Friedan tried to be a good homemaker, but she still wanted to be a writer. She faced the same decisions in the 1950s that Harriet Beecher Stowe faced in the 1850s. Should a married woman work?

Betty Friedan sold articles she wrote to magazines. She did research for a large article. She surveyed female college graduates. She asked what was their self-image? What did they want to achieve? Were they satisfied staying at home? She collected a lot of valuable information.

Friedan's book *The Feminine Mystique* was published in 1963. She changed the way women looked at themselves. Friedan said many women were not satisfied as housewives. They felt alone. Friedan said that when they found out others felt the same way, "it was such a relief . . . so empowering."[1]

A new women's group was founded in 1966. Members of the Commission on the Status of Women got the group started, and they named it the National Organization for Women (NOW).

Betty Friedan became NOW's first president. She said NOW supported "a women's movement for equality in truly equal partnership with men."[2] Another founder was Reverend Pauli Murray. She was the first African-American woman to be an Episcopal minister. Hispanic Aileen Hernandez was an early member. She became President of NOW in 1971.

NOW fought for equality for all women. In 1967, NOW pledged to "fight tirelessly for the ratification of the ERA."[3]

Women Join in Massive March

Fifty years after the suffrage amendment was passed, women

Betty Friedan

wanted to mark the anniversary. A Women's March for Equality was set in 1970 in New York City. Organizer Betty Friedan feared few women would show up. Friedan joined with leaders Bella Abzug and Gloria Steinem. They were delighted by the turnout on the day of the march. Between twenty thousand and fifty thousand marchers cheered. Many women held signs. They said "Sisterhood is Powerful!" There were also many hecklers hurling insults. Despite this, the women marched in triumph down Fifth Avenue.

Women picket during the August 26, 1970, women's rights demonstration in New York City.

Gloria Steinem

Gloria Steinem's early years in Ohio were difficult. Her mother was divorced and later became ill. The family was poor. Gloria had to be her mother's caretaker. Like her older sister Susanne, Gloria Steinem worked her way through Smith College in Massachusetts.

Steinem got a fellowship to study in India. She then struggled in New York as a writer. She wanted to write about politics, which was rare for women in the 1950s. However, Steinem wrote a startling article in 1963. She took a job as a "Bunny," a waitress at the New York Playboy Club. She revealed that the Bunnies coped with poor pay, harassment, and bad working conditions. Steinem's story made her famous.

By 1968, Steinem wrote major articles for *Esquire* magazine on American politics. She joined Bella Abzug in her Women's Strike for Peace, to protest the war in Vietnam. Together they started the National Women's Political Caucus in 1971. Steinem also began the Women's Action Alliance.

Steinem was a founder of *Ms.* magazine in 1972. *Ms.* was the first publication edited only by women. The *Ms.* staff wrote about women's rights. Steinem said: "I have met brave women who are exploring the outer edge of possibility, with no history to guide them."[4] Steinem today supports many groups that make up the women's movement.

Women Are Not in the Minority

Writer Jo Freeman published a study of working women in 1970. This study found women made up 51 percent of the American population. About 37 percent of them were in the workforce. They earned only 60 percent of what men did in the same jobs. "Women with degrees don't fare much better," said Freeman. "Only 2 percent are executives."[5] Freeman stated: "More American women die each year from medically unsafe abortions than the number of American soldiers who die annually [fighting] in Vietnam."[6]

A Difficult Legal Right Gained for Women

By 1970, women were divided by one issue. Some women believed that they should have the legal right to abort a pregnancy. Others believed abortion was wrong, even a form of murder, and must not be legal.

Laws about abortion were different in each state. The Supreme Court ruled in 1973 that abortion was legal in the first three months of pregnancy. The case was called *Roe v. Wade*. *Ms.* editor Gloria Steinem's headline screamed "NEVER AGAIN!"[7] *Ms.* meant women would never again die from getting an unsafe, illegal abortion.

Some women were not happy with this ruling. They formed groups to defend the unborn fetus. The American Right to Life Committee was founded after the *Roe v. Wade* decision was announced.[8] The debate between both sides on this legal right is as strong now as it was thirty years ago.

Title IX

Title IX was part of the Education Amendments Act passed in 1972. Title IX stated that no school getting government money could discriminate based on sex. Every school had to treat female students the same as males. Girls got the admissions, scholarships, and courses they deserved. New sports for girls were funded. Many all-male schools admitted females after Title IX.

The U.S. military service academies train officers for

the Army, Navy, Air Force, and Marines. After Title IX, they had to admit female cadets. The service branches opened up many more jobs to women than the clerical and nursing jobs they had been given before. However, women still had no right to train for a combat position.

It was estimated in a 1988 study that 11 percent of military personnel were women.[9] They were not always welcomed by males in their units, however. They had to fight for acceptance and promotion. Often, a few women were stationed with a huge number of men who resented them.

In the 1990s, women in the military moved into more dangerous and demanding positions. A U.S. Army survey

A woman trains at the Virginia Military Institute on August 20, 1997, after a court ordered the school to accept female cadets.

in 1997 said only about half of the men thought the women in their unit pulled their load, and that women were not really needed to accomplish their mission.[10] Women had to fight two battles. One was against the outside enemy. One was against the men who disliked them from inside their unit.

Equal Rights Amendment Goes to Congress

Women continued to ask their legislators to pass the Equal Rights Amendment. The Senate passed the ERA in March 1972. It read: "Equality of rights under the law shall not be denied or abridged by the United States or by any state on account of sex."[11]

Some said this amendment was not needed. Legal experts claimed that the Fourteenth Amendment (1868) already gave women equal rights. It read: "No State shall make or enforce any law which shall abridge the privileges or immunities of citizens of the United States." Would the ERA deny women privacy? Many wanted a separation between the sexes in public facilities like bathrooms.

States had to ratify this amendment by March 1979. On July 9, 1978, NOW sponsored a march in Washington. NOW asked Congress to extend the time for the states to approve the ERA. The supporters got the extension to 1982. The ERA needed thirty-eight states—three-quarters of the 50—to ratify or pass it. Just thirty-five did so in the required time frame. Once again, the ERA was not approved.

Women recalled suffragist Alice Paul. She introduced the first Equal Rights Amendment in 1923. Paul said: "We shall not be safe until the principle of equal rights is written into the framework of our government."[12]

If three more states vote yes, the ERA might yet become the Twenty-Eighth Amendment.

African Americans and Women have Similar Concerns

The fight for rights by African Americans and women brought them full circle. In 1848, women first asked for their right to vote. At that time, African Americans were slaves. Most women suffragists also tried to abolish slavery. The Civil Rights Acts of 1964 and the Age Discrimination in Employment Act of 1967 assured civil rights to women and African Americans, as well as other minorities.

All groups still needed better employment rights. The Civil Rights Act of 1991 began with: "The Congress finds that legislation is necessary to provide additional protections against unlawful discrimination in employment."[13] This act made the 1964 law stronger. Women could sue if they were denied a job because of gender.

In 1992, the U.S. Department of Labor put out a book when almost half the workforce was female. The book, *A Working Woman's Guide to her Job Rights*, said women have "equal access to all jobs for which they qualify, and equal treatment on the job."[14] However, women today are still often victims of unfair payment practices, and many continue to fight for true equal treatment in the workplace.

American Indians Are Forced to Fight

English settlers first arrived on America's shores in 1585. At that time, about six hundred Indian tribes, or about 10 million people, lived throughout North America.[1] Each group had its own language, religious customs, and elected councils. In some groups, the position of chief was passed from generation to generation. In others, the people voted for their leaders. Tribes had their own courts and punishments. For the next two hundred years, the American Indians struggled. They warred with each other and with the European intruders.

Men and women of American Indian tribes were not U.S. citizens with civil rights. They were members of their own Indian nations. In the 1780s, the founders of the United States were not even sure how many Indians lived in North America. Most white Americans lived east of the Appalachian Mountains in 1780. The western territory had never been explored.

The authors of the American Constitution considered Indians to be mainly enemies. Their goal was to control them or beat them in war. Few thought about giving them civil rights. President George Washington met with tribal leaders. He treated each group as a separate nation. Washington tried to honor agreements the Indians had made with the British.

Immigrants often arrived in America. They wanted to settle on Indian homelands. By the 1830s, Congress forced many tribes to move farther west. Indians across America fought back. They battled the U.S. Army. They were imprisoned when they lost. Conquered American Indians were forced onto smaller land areas. These areas were called "reservations."

Did Indians Have Civil Rights?

American Indians were mainly kept on their reservations. In 1871, the U.S. Congress passed the Indian Appropriation Act. It said "no Indian nation or tribe . . . shall be acknowledged or recognized as an independent nation, tribe or power with whom the United States may contract by treaty."[2] The Department of the Interior took charge of most Indian lands.

American Indians were not U.S. citizens. This meant they did not pay taxes. But they could not vote or move freely. They could not buy or sell alcohol. The government did start schools for American Indian children. However, they did not teach Indian culture or Indian languages.

In one of their last military victories, American Indians defeated General George Custer and his American troops at the Battle of the Little Bighorn in 1876. This painting of the battle was done by Charles M. Russell in 1903.

The U.S. Army Defeats American Indians

Some tribes kept fighting to stay on their lands. Still others moved to reservations. Apache leader Geronimo surrendered his band to the U.S. Army in 1886. These Apache were exhausted from fighting. The Army promised Geronimo that he would be in prison for just two years. That was a lie. Geronimo was imprisoned on an army base until he died in 1909.

Other tribes, such as the Lakota (Sioux), fought to the end. In 1890, they had a standoff at Wounded Knee Creek, South Dakota. U.S. Army troops surrounded 350 unarmed Lakota men, women, and children. The Lakota say only fifty survived the attack. The government claims that many more were alive. It was the last major fight between the Plains Indians and the U.S. Army.

American Indians Must Conform

The commissioner of Indian Affairs in 1889 set down a policy. He said Indians must "conform to the White man's ways, peaceably if they will, forceably if they must."[3] Indians lost their right to wear native costumes and hairstyles. They lost the right to speak their language. They could not practice their own religion.

This was called "forced assimilation." It meant they had to join white culture. American Indians usually did not want to join. They loved their own culture. Parents wanted to raise their children according to family tradition.

Much of the American Indians' former land was now put up for sale. The Commissioner of Indian Affairs published an advertisement in 1911. The headline read "Indian Land for Sale."[4] This land was from twelve Western states, totaling 350,000 acres. White men had the money, and they bought the land.

Author and Indian rights activist Oliver La Farge gives the example of the Flathead Indian tribe of Montana. They had 1.2 million acres allotted to them in 1908. By 1933, they had signed away 660,000 acres. The Flathead Indians owned a hydroelectric power plant. It could have irrigated their farmland. In 1925, Congress put the power plant in the hands of white men. The Bureau of Indian Affairs (BIA) was part of the U.S. Department of the Interior. This Bureau did little to help Indians.[5]

American Indian reservations were run by the BIA. The U.S. Supreme Court ruled in 1916 that if Congress chose to grant Indians citizenship, they would still be under "continued guardianship."[6]

American Indians Want Freedom of Religion

In the 1920s, Commissioner of Indian Affairs Charles H. Burke went to the Taos Pueblo in New Mexico. He told the Indians to give up their religious rituals. The Taos men refused. Burke threw them into prison. He said they violated "the Bureau's religious crimes code."[7] By 1929, the Pueblo Indians united in protest. They won the right to freedom of religion. The Department of the Interior let them alone.

American Indians Gain the Right to Citizenship

Congress passed the Indian Citizenship Act on June 2, 1924. All Indians born in the United States could be citizens.[8] Some Indians were confused. They were afraid of losing their tribal membership. Others worried they could not afford to pay taxes. Indians at least had a *choice* to become full-fledged Americans. At this time, few chose to do so.

Indian communities could not hold local elections or vote to sell their lands. Their leaders had no power. The Bureau of Indian Affairs had been little help to them. In 1933, John Collier was commissioner of the Bureau of Indian Affairs. He defended Indian ways. He worked to get an Indian rights bill passed.

In 1934, Congress passed the Indian Reorganization

Act. The government had been taking some tribes' lands in a system called "allotment." They cut it up into sections and "sold" it to each Indian family. Many of these families were unable to manage their land. Allotment was making tribes weaker. The act of 1934 stopped this practice. Also, Indian tribes could choose their own form of government. They could write their own constitutions. Indian children could attend tribal schools. Collier said of this act, "every Indian tribe might adopt it or reject it by majority vote by secret ballot."[9]

Many Indians were still poor and hungry. Jobs were scarce. Yet, they were happy to receive some control over their lives. Author/activist Oliver La Farge said they gained "the simple, democratic right possessed by every other American community."[10]

American Indian Tribes "Terminated"

American Indians had a special identity. They belonged to their tribal nation. The Indian Reorganization Act gave back rights to the tribal councils. They now felt stronger.

In 1953, Congress changed its policy. Congress said all Indians must now be citizens. They must pay taxes. They must handle their schools and health care. They must obey state laws. Special federal services were over. Indians were now on their own like white citizens. This rule was called "termination."

Termination was both good and bad for American Indians. Reservations were left with bad schools and health clinics. Many Indians had little education.

They had no way to get a job. Many were not ready to manage their lands.

An example is the Klamath tribe of Oregon. Once they controlled 21.3 million acres of timberland and ranchland. Treaties and allotments left them with a little over one million acres. Over 65 percent of the Klamaths needed government money to live. They were not taught to manage money or pay taxes. "We haven't been given that experience," said Klamath spokesman Boyd Jackson.[11] Still, the Klamath were terminated.

Tribal activists fought to have a choice. In 1958, Secretary of the Interior Fred Seaton ruled that no Indian tribe would be terminated without its consent. Now the tribes had the right to decide.

American Indians Begin to Protest

American Indians wanted more power in the 1960s. They admired African-American groups. They saw how they worked for equal rights. But Indians had problems organizing. A big issue was communicating between their native languages and English.

In 1961, the National Indian Youth Council (NIYC) was founded. These young people wanted a strong Indian identity. In 1967, Clyde Warrior (Ponca) was president of the NIYC. Warrior spoke in Memphis, Tennessee, at a hearing of the President's National Advisory Commission on Rural Poverty. He said Indians must be responsible for their lives. "The solution to Indian poverty is not 'government programs' but in the competence ... of the community as a whole," said

Warrior.[12] Russell Means (Ogallala Sioux), Dennis Banks (Ojibwa), and others founded the American Indian Movement (AIM) in 1968.

The 1968 Indian Civil Rights Act was passed. This act promised Indians the same rights given to other American citizens by the U.S. Constitution.[13] Indians would have freedom of religion, speech, and press. They were free

Russell Means led a protest during a Columbus Day Parade on October 7, 2000. Columbus Day celebrates Christopher Columbus, who Means believes ordered the killings of many Indians in the Americas.

from search and seizure. They had the right to a public jury trial with a lawyer. They would get fair bail and no cruel or unusual punishments. Finally, all men and women over twenty-one could vote in all elections.

Indian Militancy Gets Attention

On November 9, 1969, Indians took over Alcatraz Island in San Francisco Bay. On it was a deserted federal prison. Treaties said tribes could take back deserted federal land. Vine Deloria, Jr., (Standing Rock Sioux) was a legal expert. He said, "The Indians of the Bay area felt that they could lay claim to the island."[14]

Indians stayed on the island for three years. They protested against the government taking over Indian lands. Lenny Foster (Navajo) talked about being on

Alcatraz. "We got back our worth, our pride, our dignity, our humanity. If you don't have those things, then you are lost."[15]

In the winter of 1973, some members of the Pine Ridge Sioux joined AIM members Means, Banks, and others. They took over the village of Wounded Knee, South Dakota. This was the site of the 1890 massacre. The occupiers stated Wounded Knee was a separate nation. They said this was legal under a treaty of 1868.[16]

Sioux police joined with FBI agents. They tried to get the AIM protestors out of the village. Many women, children, and elderly joined the occupiers. Former chiefs and medicine men came to boost spirits. A white Roman Catholic priest, two white owners of the trading post, and about eight others were taken hostage, but they were kept safe.

Senators James Abourezk and George McGovern of South Dakota spoke to the eleven hostages. All said they supported AIM's demands. They wanted to stay.

Federal marshals surrounded the village. They had tanks and machine guns. The AIM warriors had only rifles. They were cold, hungry, and scared. Still, they did not surrender. By the end of April, electricity and running water were cut off. Shooting was frequent. A truce was reached after seventy-one days.

The standoff ended May 1, 1973. Indians had been killed. The government arrested 562 Indians with connections to AIM and the Wounded Knee takeover. They were put on trial. Their defense expenses drained all of AIM's funds.[17]

On May 17, 1973, AIM members and some Ogallalas went to Washington. They met with two aides of President Richard Nixon and other government officials. Little change in Indian policy came of it.

American Indians Try a New Venture

The Penobscots of Maine tried a new way to gain jobs and money. They opened a gambling hall. The state could not tax profits made on a reservation. Over the years more tribes decided to gamble on building casinos.

In 1988, the federal government passed the Indian

An AIM member at Wounded Knee celebrates news of an extension of a ceasefire between the government and AIM members.

Gaming Regulatory Act. Tribal leaders began making gambling agreements with state governments. Today, some American Indians think that reservation gambling casinos could be the wave of the future for tribal financial security.

Rights for Latinos

One of the first Europeans to land in North America was Spanish. Ponce de Leon explored the Florida shores in 1513. Hernandez de Cordoba explored further in 1517. Soon Spaniards founded many towns. They settled the southeast and southwest of America. St. Augustine, Florida, was the first permanent settlement. The Spanish made it a fort in 1565. The next year, Martin de Arguella was the first European baby born in America.[1]

Mexico was settled in the 1540s by Spain. Hernan Cortes discovered the lower California peninsula. This is part of Mexico today. Juan Rodriguez Cabrillo, a Portuguese sailor, explored the California coast for Spain in 1542.

Later, the Catholic Church sent priests. They built many missions and tried to convert American Indians to their Christian faith. Mexicans settled much of present-day California.

By the twenty-first century, Mexicans had become the largest group of Hispanic descent in America. In the 2000 census, 20.6 million people, or 58 percent of Latinos, were Mexican Americans.[2] Many of them first lived in Texas, New Mexico, Arizona, and California. Until 1848, these areas were part of Mexico.

The U.S. government battled Mexico for these territories. The U.S. armed forces won. Mexicans in these areas suddenly became Mexican Americans. "Anglos" ruled them. This was their term for English-speaking white Americans. Anglo-Americans had new styles, customs, and language. Mexican Americans had become "foreigners in their own land."[3]

Other Latino Groups Arrive

Cubans immigrated to Florida in the 1950s and 1960s. The immigrants opposed Fidel Castro's communist rule in their country. Most of these Cubans were educated. They received money from the state of Florida but they also worked hard. They did not want to return to Cuba.

Puerto Ricans also immigrated during the twentieth century. Their island became a territory of the United States in 1898. They became U.S. citizens in 1917. After that, Puerto Ricans could move freely back and forth without a passport.

Many Puerto Ricans came to New York City. From 1900 to 1945, men and women got jobs there in the textile and garment factories. The men also worked as cigar makers. After World War II, a large number of Puerto Ricans began living in New Jersey and Connecticut.

By 1969, about eight hundred thousand Puerto Ricans had moved to the U.S. mainland.[4] They became the largest Latino group in the Northeast. By the start of the twenty-first century, almost 3.4 million people

Puerto Ricans demonstrate for better education and housing in New York City.

on the mainland were of Puerto Rican descent.[5]

In the 2000 U.S. census, Latinos were able to mark their origins. They could check Mexican (58.5 percent), Puerto Rican (9.6 percent), or Cuban (3.5 percent). Other choices were South American (3.8 percent) and Central American (4.8 percent). In the last group, El Salvador, Nicaragua, and Guatemala had the largest number. Another choice was "all other Hispanic" (17.6 percent). The total Latinos counted were 35.3 million.[6] (This count did not include the 3.8 million Puerto Rican residents living in the territory of Puerto Rico.) By 2002, the total Latino population had risen to 38.8 million.[7]

Latinos Face Job Discrimination

Mexican Americans had to work for Anglo-American bosses. They were hired as ranch hands in Texas. They were miners in New Mexico. They took low-skilled laborer and farm jobs in California. From 1850 to 1950, jobs did not improve much for these workers.

Historian Ronald Takaki noted that when Mexican

Americans did the same job as an Anglo, they were still paid less. He told of a study made around 1900. Mexican-American silver miners were paid between $12 and $30 a month. Anglo miners got between $30 and $70. Mexican Americans were stuck in poverty. They had to buy food and clothes from company stores. They were "chained to the company," much like African-American sharecroppers were to the land they farmed.[8]

By 1901, Mexican Americans had begun to strike. Construction workers struck in El Paso, Texas. Miners struck in Thurber, Texas. Farmworkers struck in Oxnard, California. They wanted the same wage as whites. They wanted job security and medical care. Other Mexican-American families stood by those on strike. They gave food, clothes, and services. This united effort worked. In most cases, the striking Mexicans won.

Many Mexican Americans moved to cities. They learned to speak English. Still, they hit a wall. Anglo-Americans kept them in low-paying factory or laborer positions. No offices or banks would hire a Mexican American.

Latina women were offered jobs as housekeepers, maids, and servants. They also took hard jobs in canneries and fish processing plants. Their wages were kept low. Latino farmworkers were scattered all through the South and West. These Latinos were poorly paid. They had very little schooling because they were migrants. They moved as the crops needed harvesting. How could they unite?

Cesar Chavez

Cesar Chavez was born in 1927 in Arizona. His parents were Mexican-American. The family moved to California. They were fruit pickers. Chavez skipped high school to work. Later he married and had eight children. His dream was to organize the farmworkers. In 1962 he founded a labor group. It became the United Farm Workers (UFW).

Chavez used the same kind of marches and boycotts as Martin Luther King. He also fasted. He led a 340-mile march to Sacramento. He encouraged people to boycott lettuce and grapes, until growers allowed the union. His union grew stronger. By 1971, Chavez and the UFW won contracts from food-growing companies.

Chavez wrote in 1985: "Some farmworkers now earn fair pay and have family medical plans, protection from dangerous pesticides, and paid holidays. . . . their children attend school and they make enough to live in decent homes instead of wretched camps."[9]

Chavez also protested the use of pesticides on grapes, lettuce, and other produce. Too many chemicals made farmworkers sick. He spoke out against pesticides in 1989. Chavez demanded: "What is the worth of a farm worker? How do you measure the value of a life?"[10] Chavez died in his sleep in 1993. The UFW lives on as a tribute to his work for equal rights.

Latinos Struggle to Vote

Latinos had a hard time getting to vote. They usually lived together in poor neighborhoods. Adults and children read and spoke mostly Spanish. Latinos got their news from Spanish newspapers and radio stations. In this way they learned about candidates for office.

However, all instructions were in English at voting places. In some areas, Latinos had to take an English reading test. Most got discouraged. They did not vote.

The Southwest Voter Registration and Education Project (SVREP) was formed in 1974. SVREP helped Mexican Americans throughout Texas, Arizona, and California understand the issues. They could now figure out how the American voting system worked.[11]

After the Voting Rights Act of 1965, fees and reading tests were not legal. By 1975, the Voting Rights Act was made broader. It stated that in areas where more than 5 percent of voters spoke one other language, information and ballots must be offered in that language.

The U.S. Department of Justice listed states under this new rule. Alaska, Arizona, and Texas were covered. Much of California, Florida, Michigan, New York, North Carolina, and South Dakota also had to comply.[12]

The DOJ does not state which language was covered. The "single language minority" in Alaska and South Dakota was the American Indian. The other states put out voting information in Spanish. This act helped thousands of Latinos register and vote.

Willie Velasquez, a member of the Southwest Voter Registration and Education Project, helps a fellow Hispanic man register to vote.

Segregation and Affirmative Action Affect Latinos

Segregation in schools was against the law after 1954. Mexican-American, Cuban, and Puerto Rican children were allowed to go to any public school. However, most of these children ended up living in segregated neighborhoods. They called these areas "barrios" in Spanish. There were many reasons why Latinos lived in barrios. It was easier to shop and get along when everyone around you spoke your language.

An example of this is Los Angeles, California. The Los Angeles Unified School District said in 1999 that 69 percent of its students were Latinos. Half did not speak English well. Almost 75 percent got free lunch services, based on income level.[13]

The Bureau of the Census did a survey in 1999. It found that 50 percent of Mexican Americans, 36.1 percent of Puerto Ricans, 29 percent of Cubans, and 36 percent of South Americans did not finish high school.[14]

Many Latinos are impoverished or have trouble speaking English. They need special help in school. Over half of Latinos live in California and Texas. Affirmative Action laws were rejected by voters there, eliminating a program that helped Latino students get into college.

Should Latino Children be Taught in Spanish?

For several decades, people have argued whether teachers should speak Spanish in public schools. If lessons are taught in both English and Spanish, the school is called "bilingual." This means two languages. There is no state that has ruled for or against teaching in Spanish. Parents and teachers are divided. Latino parents in the Los Angeles Unified School District were asked, and a large majority wanted bilingual schooling. Many schools have chosen an ESL, or English as a Second Language, program. Students who do not speak English well go to an ESL class. They get this special help several times a day. The rest of the day, they go through school in English.

Because of the language barrier, getting a good education is the single largest challenge facing Latinos in America today.

Rights for Asians and People with Disabilities

Chinese Americans arrived in America in the early nineteenth century. They came because of wars and poverty in China. They hoped to send money back home.

These Chinese Americans were almost all men. Many were too poor to get married in China. Married men asked their wives to wait. In the Chinese culture, women stayed in the home. They cared for children and grandparents. The men knew they would be doing hard labor in a strange land. There would be no room for their families.

Discrimination Starts Against Miners

Gold was discovered in California in 1848. After ten years, more than forty thousand Chinese-American men were mining for gold. These men worked night and day. Other miners were biased against them. California passed a special "miner's tax." It targeted Chinese Americans only.

San Francisco was home to many Chinese Americans. Whites resented them. The city passed a "hair-cutting ordinance."[1] Chinese men wore a long braid down their back that showed they were loyal Chinese. This law forced them to cut their braid. The men were humiliated. Later, Chinese Americans could not attend public school. Yet they stayed.

White bandits attacked Chinese gold miners. They stole the claims to their mines. Some Chinese Americans stopped mining and started businesses. Laundries were needed. They were easy to start up. Families could now come over from China to join the men. "Chinese wash-houses were a common sight as early as the 1850s," said historian Ronald Takaki.[2]

In 1865, the Central Pacific Railroad was begun. This railroad track was to run east from Sacramento, California, and would join up with another railroad line coming toward it. The railroad company needed many laborers. Company president Leland Stanford looked to China.

Chinese Americans began blasting through the Sierra Mountains. They then laid track. According to a PBS film called *The Chinese Experience*, "approximately 11,000 Chinese men were recruited."[3] Others already in California joined the railroad gangs.

These Chinese Americans were paid less than white laborers. They still did this dangerous job well. Stanford stated: "If it weren't for the Chinese we could not be building this railroad."[4]

Members of a construction crew, some of them Chinese, pose on a handcar on the Union Pacific Railroad.

Excluded From Immigration

Chinese Americans worked in cities throughout the West. They also worked as Latinos did, picking farm produce. In 1880, there was a job shortage. White laborers directed their anger at the Chinese immigrants.

U.S. President Rutherford B. Hayes called the Chinese "an invasion." He said: "I would consider with favor any suitable measures" to stop Chinese people from coming to America.[5] Congress passed the Chinese Exclusion Act of 1882. This act kept Chinese people out. No other ethnic group had been outlawed in this way.

In 1898, a case called *Wong Kim Ark v. U.S.* went to the U.S. Supreme Court. Wong Kim Ark had been denied entry into the United States, despite the fact that he had been born there in 1873. The Court affirmed that anyone born in the United States is a citizen according to the Constitution. Those with citizenship could bring over family members from China.

The Chinese Exclusion Act was repealed on December 17, 1943. This ended more than sixty years of discrimination. These exclusion laws had "affected generations of Chinese immigrants."[6]

Why did America repeal this act? This was in the middle of World War II. Young men in China were being trained in science and technology. The American military wanted them to come. They put them in defense industries. Also, China had become an ally of the United States. The U.S. could not exclude allies from immigrating. The needs of the war were more important than racial bias. From then on, the Chinese American population grew.

In 1965, the federal government passed the Immigration and Nationality Act. This act let Chinese Americans become naturalized citizens. They could join other ethnic groups and enjoy full rights as Americans.

Japanese Americans Become American Farmers

By 1900, Japanese were moving to the Western states of America. A study proved that about thirty thousand Japanese-American men were working on farms by 1909.[7] These men pooled their money. They began to lease or buy their own farms.

In California, white farmers resented Japanese Americans. They got an Alien Land Bill passed in 1913. It said "Japanese aliens" could lease for only three years. The state's attorney general said: "they will not come in large numbers and long abide with us if they may not acquire land."[8]

Japanese Americans left farming and became gardeners and landscapers. They worked for white owners. They went into trades and opened businesses. Their immigration was not limited like that of Chinese Americans.

That changed in 1924. Japanese Americans were turned away from America. They would not be able to immigrate again until 1952.

Japanese Face Discrimination due to World War II

Japanese-American residents did well. Their families grew. By 1940, there were more that 126,000 on the American mainland, and 157,000 in the territory of Hawaii.[9] On the whole, Japanese Americans were loyal and successful citizens. After the Japanese attack on Pearl Harbor on December 7, 1941, Japan became America's enemy in war.

Japanese Americans did not support the Emperor of Japan. Still, they paid the price for being of that ethnicity. The Japanese Americans living in the Western states were considered enemies who could not be trusted.

This did not happen in the territory of Hawaii. The War Department wanted the Japanese taken away and put in camps. General Delos Emmons was the Military Governor on Hawaii. He refused. He said these citizens were loyal. Besides, they were one-third of Hawaii's population. To lose them would destroy the workforce. Almost all these Japanese Americans kept their jobs.

The Japanese Americans in the Western states were a smaller percent of those states' total population. Their labor was not as necessary. President Franklin D. Roosevelt gave in to military commanders. He violated the Constitution. He issued an executive order that put all Japanese-American citizens from the west coast into internment camps.[10]

Soldiers forced the Japanese Americans onto old military bases. They were in remote areas of seven Western states. Living in these desolate army barracks was harsh. After a year, about thirty-five thousand Japanese Americans got out. Teenagers went to college. Some young adults found jobs in the Midwest and East. The families who were kept in the camps were ruined. They never got their money or property back.

Many Japanese Americans proved their loyalty. They joined the U.S. armed forces. World War II ended in May 1945. When one unit of Japanese-American soldiers came home, they had more decorations for valor

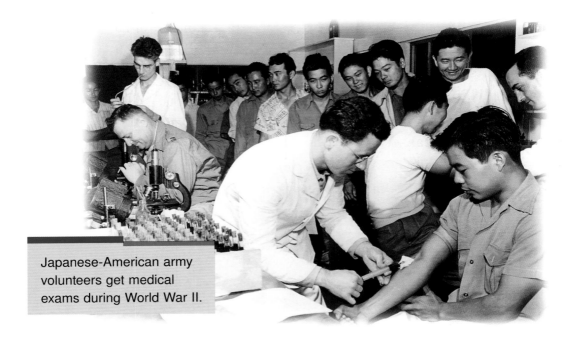

Japanese-American army volunteers get medical exams during World War II.

than almost any other. President Harry Truman welcomed them. He said, "you fought not only the enemy, you fought prejudice—and you won."[11]

Many Japanese Americans demanded some repayment. By 1976, the government admitted it had made a mistake. In 1988, President Ronald Reagan signed the Civil Liberties Act. This bill said that it had been wrong to imprison Japanese Americans. It was done because of racism. Each camp survivor got a payment. It came to twenty thousand dollars per person.[12]

People with Disabilities Get their Rights

A certain group from both sexes and all races still needed help. They faced discrimination in education and jobs. Doors and stairs kept them out. These people had a "disability." The government defines a disability as "a physical or mental impairment that substantially limits one or more major life activities."[13] According to the National Organization on Disability (NOD), 54 million Americans are in this group. They fought for equal rights for many years.

People with disabilities finally won their rights. They were covered under the Americans with Disabilities Act of 1990 (ADA). By July 1992, companies with twenty-five or more employees had to give people with disabilities a job, if they could perform it. Workplaces had to be open to people in wheelchairs and walkers.

The ADA helped people with disabilities pursue a career. It said they could enter businesses and workplaces like everyone else. They should have access to schools, public places, and even bathrooms. Ramps and lifts help them with transportation. Only places of worship do not have to comply.

John Hockenberry is a news reporter and commentator who has traveled the world to cover stories. He is a speaker and author. He also must use a wheelchair. Hockenberry says that many places of worship do comply, "because it is the right thing to do."[14]

Captioned television and text phones help the hearing impaired. Large-print books, Braille and audio books, and special computers help the visually impaired. Hockenberry says: "that disabled people have certain rights that cannot be denied . . . there is a place for all in America."[15]

Have We Overcome?

An anthem of the African-American civil rights movement is "We Shall Overcome," an old spiritual. The dream expressed in the song is that everyone will someday have the civil rights they deserve. By the twenty-first century, the dream should have come true.

Women Have Special Issues

New mothers cannot be fired for taking a leave from their jobs. The Family and Medical Leave Act (FMLA) went into effect in August 1993. The FMLA grants a woman who gives birth or adopts a baby twelve weeks of unpaid leave from her job. Leave can also be used to care for a seriously ill child, spouse, or parent. The employer must give the worker health care during the leave and hold her job open. Some states allow a leave for the new fathers as well.

In some cases, women do not get equal pay for equal work. In 2004, the Institute for Women's Policy Research stated: "Women earned about 76 cents on the dollar earned by men."[1] This figure came from the U.S. Census Bureau. In America, the average salary per year for a woman was $30,724. The average salary for a man per year was $40,668.

Women can sometimes take twelve weeks of unpaid leave to care for a baby.

There are several reasons for this gap. Many women are not getting the higher paying jobs in "male" fields. They are not training for them or applying for them. If hired, and they need to take time off for family care, they do not get promoted.

The Institute for Women's Policy Research stated, "it will take 50 more years before women's paychecks will equal men's."[2] The Institute asked that equal opportunity laws be strongly enforced.

Harassment on the Job is Wrong

Making unwanted advances toward someone at work is wrong. Speaking to or touching a person in an unwelcome sexual way is called harassment. Harassment is discrimination. It has been against the law since Title VII of the Civil Rights Act of 1964. Women were especially affected by sexual harassment, yet few of them filed charges. They were afraid of being

"I am terribly careful with my vote."

—Irma Gotsch Schmidt, who has voted in every election since women gained the right to vote.

ridiculed or embarrassed. They thought they would lose their job. They feared male judges would rule against them. More women today protest this harassment and often file legal charges if they are victim to it.

Today's Women Have Come a Long Way

Many women of all races appreciate the right to vote. On November 3, 2004, Irma Gotsch Schmidt of Farmington, Connecticut, voted. At the time, she was 106 years old. She had voted in every presidential election since the Constitutional Amendment in 1920.

In 1920, when she first voted, Schmidt joined her whole family to vote in their Ohio town. Her grandmother was thrilled. She told Irma: "I never thought I'd live long enough to see the vote."[3] Schmidt prepared for each election. She studied the newspapers and looked at history. "I am terribly careful with my vote," she said.

The U.S. Department of State included this statistic

in its April 2004 newsletter: "According to the U.S. Census Bureau, 61 percent of eligible women voters cast a ballot in the 2000 presidential election."[4] Unfortunately, that means almost 40 percent of eligible women did *not* vote. However, women have continued to fight for their rights. National Organization of Women founder Betty Friedan died in 2006. Members of NOW mourned her, but still advocate for women in the spirit of their founder.

African-American Victories and Struggles

African Americans remember the struggle for voting rights and integrated schools. It lives in the hearts of those who survived. Vertia Killings is from Tuscaloosa, Alabama. She spoke about her African-American father trying to vote. When she was a girl in the 1930s, African Americans had to pay a poll tax. She said her father paid forty-five dollars. This was a lot of money then, so Killings' family had less to eat. Other men, she said, chose to eat instead of vote.

Killings remembered when schools became integrated. She says: "It seems like we're having a reversal."[5] African-American city children are having a hard time finding an integrated public school. This is because white families mostly live in the suburbs and small towns. Many can afford to send their children to private school, and some even teach them at home. Many of America's urban schools are becoming segregated again.

American Indians Are Gambling on their Future

Unemployment is still a major issue for American Indians. Reservation casinos, hotels, and resorts do provide jobs. However, they are getting mixed receptions. It remains to be seen if gambling casinos will help bring real prosperity and unity to American Indians. Tribes such as the Mohegans and the Mashantucket Pequots of Connecticut have enormous gaming resorts. Profits have put these American Indians in a strong position. Other tribes have resisted casinos on their lands. The largest tribe, the Navajo, has refused to allow gaming.

Ojibwa Jim Northrup worked on his reservation's casino in Fond du Lac, Minnesota. He said in 1997 that each member of his tribe earned only about fifteen hundred dollars a year from casino profits. Northrup said the casino "has brought our Rez [reservation] unemployment rate from 80 percent all the way down to 50 percent."[6]

Latinos Strive to Live Well

The number of people who identify themselves as Latino in America keeps growing. More people want to immigrate from Mexico, and Central and South America. However, there are rules on how many can come. So many immigrate illegally.

Farmworkers still have their unions to help them get equal pay and respect. Life can be harder for urban Latinos. Gangs and criminal groups disrupt their communities. Latinos often get jobs with low pay and no benefits. Yet they enjoy equal protection under the law.

Education and language issues have not been overcome. However, the situation for Hispanic youths has improved. In 2002, the high school dropout rate for Latinos/Hispanics was 33.8 percent for males and 25.6 percent for females. This was down from 36.4 percent for males and 31.1 percent for females in 1999. About 53 percent of those who graduated high school went on to enroll in college or take some college courses. This was up from 50 percent in 1999.[7] Some Latinos have achieved high positions in America. They are lawyers, mayors, legislators, and company owners.

Asian Groups Gain Strength

Asians have come to America throughout the twentieth century. There are also people from Korea, Vietnam,

Asian-Americans rarely drop out of school because of strong family support.

Laos, Cambodia, the Philippines, and Thailand. Each group has tried to stick together. They support each other and new immigrants from their home country. They enjoy the freedom to practice their own religion and their culture.

Urban Asians suffer some of the same problems as urban Latinos. They live on low salaries and can be involved in gangs. Very strong family pressure and support keeps Asians in school. Their high school dropout rate is just 4 percent. Of Asian graduates, 65.3 percent go to college, the highest rate of any ethnic group.[8]

Liberty and Justice for All?

For fifty years, a famous judge presided over the U.S. Court of Appeals, Second Circuit. His name was Learned Hand. Judge Hand was asked about liberty and justice for all. What did he think "liberty" was?

It is not the freedom to do what you like, said Judge Hand. Liberty "seeks to understand the mind of other men and women . . . without bias," he said. "Liberty lies in the hearts of men and women; when it dies there, no constitution, no law, no court can even do much to help it."[9]

Americans have been assured civil rights by the law. Yet the spirit of justice, as Judge Learned Hand says, must lie in the heart of every citizen. Each person, no matter what race or gender or ethnic background, must respect all others. Then America will have truly achieved equal rights.

1791 The Bill of Rights, the first ten amendments to the Constitution, was passed.

1830 Removal Act. All Indian tribes east of the Mississippi River were to move to western territories and give up their lands for sale.

1848 First women's rights meeting was held in Seneca Falls, New York, in July.

1850 The Fugitive Slave Law, stating that all free states must give up escaped slaves, was passed.

1852 *Uncle Tom's Cabin* by Harriet Beecher Stowe was published, inspiring a push for the abolition of slavery.

1857 The reservation system for Indians was created. Indians were given enough land to grow crops but not enough to hunt.

1865 The Civil War ended. The Confederacy surrendered on April 9. The Thirteenth Amendment to the Constitution was passed, freeing all slaves. The Central Pacific Railroad is built mainly by Chinese men.

1866 A Civil Rights Act passed, giving black men the same rights as white men.

1868 The Fourteenth Amendment to the Constitution was passed, guaranteeing that all persons born or naturalized in the United States are citizens and that no state can take away the privileges of a citizen.

1869 National Woman Suffrage Association (NWSA) and

American Woman Suffrage Association (AWSA) are both founded. Their agenda: get women the vote.

1870 Fifteenth Amendment to the Constitution was passed, declaring that all [male] citizens of legal age cannot be denied the vote because of race, color, or previous slavery.

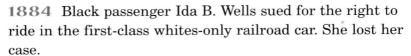

1875 A Civil Rights Act was passed. Discrimination by race was against the law.

1882 Chinese Exclusion Act was passed to stop Chinese immigration.

1884 Black passenger Ida B. Wells sued for the right to ride in the first-class whites-only railroad car. She lost her case.

1890 Wyoming was the first state to allow women residents to vote. U.S. Army battles the Lakota at Wounded Knee, South Dakota. The Lakota were wiped out.

1896 In *Plessy v. Ferguson*, black passenger Homer Plessy sued for the right to ride in a first-class whites-only railroad car. The Supreme Court ruled that the black car was "separate but equal."

1909 The National Association for the Advancement of Colored People (NAACP) was founded.

1910 First parade for women's suffrage was held in New York City.

1914 National Women's Party was founded by Alice Paul.

1917 African Americans served in segregated units in

World War I. More than six hundred were commissioned as officers. Puerto Ricans became U.S. citizens.

1920 The Nineteenth Amendment to the Constitution was ratified by the needed thirty-six states, giving women the right to vote.

1917–1921 Each summer, race riots exploded in American cities.

1921 First attempt made to pass an Equal Rights Amendment for women.

1924 Indian Citizenship Act was passed. All Indians could be U.S. citizens if they chose.

1930 The Nation of Islam (NOI) was founded. The Black Muslim movement began.

Margaret Sanger

1934 Indian Reorganization Act turned form of government back to tribes.

1941 America declared war on Japan and its allies. One million women took defense-related jobs as men were drafted.

1942 Congress of Racial Equality (CORE) was founded. Japanese Americans were interned at old military bases throughout the United States.

1943 Chinese Exclusion Act was repealed. Chinese could immigrate and be naturalized.

1948 President Harry S. Truman signed the Executive Order to end segregation and inequality in the military.

1954 In *Brown v. Board* of Education, segregation in schools was declared unconstitutional.

1955 Rosa Parks refused to go to the back of the bus and the Montgomery, Alabama, boycott began.

1957 President Dwight D. Eisenhower signed a Civil Rights Act to enforce integration and voting registration rights.

1961 Freedom Rides were met with violence in the South.

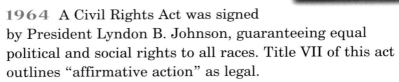

1962 Cesar Chavez and others form the United Farm Workers Union to help migrant laborers.

1963 Martin Luther King, Jr., led a March to the Lincoln Memorial in August. President John F. Kennedy was assassinated on November 22.

1964 A Civil Rights Act was signed by President Lyndon B. Johnson, guaranteeing equal political and social rights to all races. Title VII of this act outlines "affirmative action" as legal.

1965 A Voting Rights Act outlawed reading tests for voters.

1966 National Organization for Women (NOW) was founded.

1967 Race riots tore apart large American cities.

1968 Martin Luther King, Jr., was murdered. American Indian Movement (AIM) was founded to fight for Indian rights. Indian Civil Rights Act was passed, assuring the same civil rights as in Bill of Rights.

1969 A group of Indians occupied Alcatraz Island and its deserted federal prison.

1970 Women's March for Equality in New York City celebrated 50 years of the vote.

1971 Bella Abzug, Gloria Steinem, and other feminist leaders founded the National Women's Political Caucus.

1972 Education Amendments Act was passed in 1972. Title IX gave equal treatment in all areas to female students as to males. Shirley Chisholm, an African-American woman, runs for president.

1973 The Supreme Court ruling in *Roe v. Wade* made getting an abortion legal. AIM members join with Lakotas and occupy the village of Wounded Knee, South Dakota.

1975 Voting Rights Act was passed. Areas with more than 5 percent of voters speaking a language other than

Shirley Chisholm

English could get information and ballots in that language.

1990 Americans with Disabilities Act was passed, assuring job and access rights to the disabled.

1991 A Civil Rights Act was passed to protect women and minorities from unlawful discrimination in employment.

Chapter One Rosa Parks Worked for Equal Rights

1. Douglas Brinkley, *Rosa Parks* (New York: Viking/Penguin Putnam, Inc., 2000), p. 88.
2. Ibid., p. 100.
3. Rosa Parks, with Jim Haskins, *Rosa Parks: My Story* (New York: Dial/Penguin, 1992), p. 114.
4. Ibid., p. 117.
5. Ibid., pp. 122, 126.
6. "Rosa Parks: How I Fought for Civil Rights: Arrested," *Culture & Change: Black History in America*, n.d., <http://teacher.scholastic.com/rosa/arrested.htm> (October 4, 2005).
7. Parks and Haskins, pp. 126–127.
8. Brinkley, p. 115.
9. Parks and Haskins, p. 77.
10. Brinkley, p. 130.
11. Rosa Parks, with Gregory J. Reed, *Quiet Strength: The Faith, the Hope and the Heart of a Woman Who Changed a Nation* (Grand Rapids, Mich.: Zondervan Publishing House/HarperCollins, 1994), p. 26.

Chapter Two Rights of Americans in the Constitution

1. "Declaration of Independence," *ushistory.org*, n.d., <http://www.ushistory.org/declaration/document/index.htm> (October 3, 2005).
2. James Madison, "To Thomas Jefferson, October 17, 1788," *Constitution Society*, n.d., <http://www.constitution.org/jm/17881017_tj.htm> (November 7, 2005).
3. "The Bill of Rights," *Archiving Early America—America's Freedom Documents*, n.d., <http://www.earlyamerica.com/earlyamerica/freedom/bill/index.html> (November 7, 2005).

Chapter Three African Americans Living in Slavery

1. Ira Berlin, *Slaves Without Masters*, quoted in "Free Persons of Color in Charleston Before the Civil War. Earning a Living as a Free Black in Charleston," *SCIway.net*, n.d., <http://www.sciway.net/hist/chicora/freepersons-2.html> (October 4, 2005).
2. John Hope Franklin and Alfred A. Moss, Jr., *From Slavery to Freedom. A History of African Americans*, 8th edition (New York: McGraw Hill, 2000), p. 171.

3. William W. Freehling, *The Reintegration of American History: Slavery and the Civil War* (New York: Oxford University Press, 1994), p. 140.

4. Geoffrey C. Ward, with Ken Burns and Ric Burns, *The Civil War* (New York: Alfred A. Knopf, 1990), pp. 25–26.

5. Joan D. Hedrick, *Harriet Beecher Stowe, A Life* (New York: Oxford University Press, 1994), p. 208.

6. Sarah H. Bradford, *Harriet Tubman: The Moses of Her People* (Bedford, Mass.: Applewood Books, 1993), p. 22.

7. Ibid., p. 30.

8. "Forty Acres and a Mule: Primary Sources," *American Experience: Reconstruction: The Second Civil War*, 1999–2003 PBS Online/WGBH, <http://www.pbs.org/wgbh/amex/reconstruction/40acres/ps_so15.html> (October 4, 2005).

9. Ronald Takaki, A *Different Mirror: A History of Multicultural America* (New York: Little Brown and Company, 1993), p. 135.

10. Frederick Douglass, "My Bondage and My Freedom," in *The Frederick Douglass Papers: Autobiographical Writing*, series 2, vol. 2, eds. John W. Blassingame, John R. McKivigan, and Peter P. Hinks (New Haven, Conn.: Yale University Press, 2003), p. 31.

11. Nick Treanor, ed., *The Civil Rights Movement* (San Diego: The Gale Group, 2003), p. 33.

12. David W. Blight, *Frederick Douglass' Civil War* (Baton Rouge: Louisiana State University Press, 1989), p. 191.

13. Franklin and Moss, pp. 250–251.

14. James M. McPherson, *Ordeal by Fire: The Civil War and Reconstruction* (New York: McGraw-Hill Company, 2001), p. 618.

Chapter Four   African Americans Are Kept Separate by State Laws

1. W. Haywood Burns, *The Voices of Negro Protest in America* (Westport, Conn.: Greenwood Press, Publishers, 1980), p. 7.

2. Joel Williamson, ed., *The Origins of Segregation* (Boston: D.C. Heath and Company, 1968), p. 15.

3. Ronald L. F. Davis, Ph.D., "Creating Jim Crow: In-Depth Essay," *The History of Jim Crow*, n.d., <http://jimcrowhistory.org/history/creating2.htm> (October 5, 2005).

4. Burns, p. 18.

5. Mildred I. Thompson, *Ida B. Wells-Barnett: An Exploratory Study of an American Black Woman, 1893–1930* (Brooklyn, N.Y.: Carlson Publishing, Inc., 1990), p. 20.

6. Philip A. Klinkner with Rogers M. Smith, *The Unsteady March: The Rise and Decline of Racial Equality in America* (Chicago: University of Chicago Press, 1999), p. 111.

7. "World War I and Post War Society, Part 1: Fighting at Home and Abroad," *African American Odyssey: A Quest for Full Citizenship*, n.d., <http://memory.loc.gov/ammem/aaohtml/exhibit/aopart7.html> (October 5, 2005).

8. Gerald C. Hynes, "A Biographical Sketch of *W.E.B. DuBois,*" *W.E.B. DuBois Learning Center*, n.d., <http://www.duboislc.org/man.html> (October 4, 2005).

9. "Lynching," *Spartacus Educational*, n.d., <http://www.spartacus.schoolnet.co.uk/USAlynching.htm> (November 4, 2005).

10. "1919: Race Riots," *Chicago Public Library: Deaths, Disturbances, Disasters and Disorders in Chicago*, April 2005, <http://www.chipublib.org/004chicago/disasters/riots_race.html> (November 7, 2005).

11. Mark Bauerlein, et al., *Civil Rights Chronicle: The African-American Struggle for Freedom* (Legacy Publishing, 2003), p. 48.

12. Meyer Weinberg, ed., *W.E.B. Du Bois: A Reader* (New York: Harper & Row, Publishers, 1970), p. 104.

13. "The Tulsa Race Riot of 1921," *The Tulsa Library: African-American Resource Center*, n.d., <http://www.tulsalibrary.org/aarc/Riot/riot.htm> (November 7, 2005).

14. Bauerlein, et al., p. 65.

15. Ibid., p. 66.

16. John Henrik Clarke, "The New Afro-American Nationalism," *Let Freedom Ring: A Documentary History of the Modern Civil Rights Movement*, ed., Peter B. Levy (New York: Praeger Publishers, 1992), pp. 27–28.

17. James Farmer, "Tolstoi and Tolson," *Lay Bare the Heart*, n.d., <http://sunrisedancer.com/radicalreader/library/laybaretheheart/srclaybeartheheart11.asp> (November 7, 2005).

18. A. Philip Randolph, "Keynote Address to the March on Washington Movement," *Let Freedom Ring: A Documentary History of the Modern Civil Rights Movement*, ed. Peter B. Levy (New York: Praeger Publishers, 1992), pp. 13–14.

19. Raymond H. Geselbracht, "The Truman Administration, and the Desegregation of the Armed Forces: A Chronology," *Truman Presidential Library and Museum*, n.d., <http://www.trumanlibrary.org/deseg1> (September 29, 2005).

20. Harry S. Truman, *Memoirs*, vol. 2, "Years of Trial and Hope" (New York: Doubleday and Company, 1956), p. 184.

Chapter Five   Segregated Schools Are *Not* Equal

1. Meyer Weinberg, ed., *W.E.B. Du Bois: A Reader* (New York: Harper & Row, Publishers, 1970), pp. 143–144.

2. Mark Bauerlein, et al., *Civil Rights Chronicle:*

The African-American Struggle for Freedom (Legacy Publishing, 2003), p. 72.

3. Ibid., p. 121.
4. President Dwight D. Eisenhower, "Address on Little Rock," *Let Freedom Ring: A Documentary History of the Modern Civil Rights Movement*, ed. Peter B. Levy (New York: Praeger Publishers, 1992), pp. 47–48.
5. Ibid., p. 74.
6. James Peck, *Freedom Ride* (New York: Simon & Schuster, 1962), pp. 78–79.
7. Martin Luther King, Jr., *I Have a Dream: Writings and Speeches that Changed the World*, ed. James Melvin Washington (San Francisco: Harper San Francisco, 1986), p. 88.
8. Ibid., p. 104.
9. Charles and Barbara Whalen, *The Longest Debate: A Legislative History of the 1964 Civil Rights Act* (Washington, D.C.: Seven Locks Press, 1985), p. 237.
10. Lyndon B. Johnson, "Address Before a Joint Session of Congress," *Let Freedom Ring: A Documentary History of the Modern Civil Rights Movement*, ed. Peter B. Levy (New York: Praeger Publishers, 1992), p. 159.
11. Bauerlein, et al., p. 338.
12. Hugh Davis Graham, "Race, History, and Policy: African Americans and Civil Rights Since 1964," *The Civil Rights Movement*, ed. Jack E. Davis (Malden, Mass.: Blackwell Publishers, 2001), p. 287.
13. Richard Nixon, *Richard Nixon: The Memoirs of Richard Nixon* (New York: Grosset & Dunlap, 1978), p. 437
14. Jo Ann Ooiman Robinson, ed., *Affirmative Action: A Documentary History* (Westport, Conn.: Greenwood Press, 2001), p. 294.
15. Ibid.
16. Ibid., p. 313.

Chapter Six   Women Are Not Treated Equally

1. Lois W. Banner, *Elizabeth Cady Stanton, A Radical for Woman's Rights* (Boston: Little, Brown and Company, 1980), p. 43.
2. Paulina W. Davis and Victoria C. Woodhull, *A History of the National Woman's Rights Movement for Twenty Years* (New York: Kraus Reprint Co., 1971, ©1871), p. 7.
3. Ibid., p. 46.
4. Jone Johnson Lewis, "Lucy Stone Quotations," *About Women's History*, ©2005, <http://womenshistory.about.com/library/qu/blquston.htm> (November 7, 2005).
5. Ibid., p. 5.

6. "National Woman Suffrage Association," *Women in American History by Encyclopedia Britannica*, ©1999, <http://search.eb.com/women/articles/National_Woman_Suffrage_Association.html> (November 7, 2005).
7. Davis and Woodhull, p. 50.
8. Barbara Goldsmith, *Other Powers: The Age of Suffrage, Spiritualism, and the Scandalous Victoria Woodhull* (New York: Alfred A. Knopf, 1998), p. 52.
9. Mary Gabriel, *Notorious Victoria: The Life of Victoria Woodhull, Uncensored* (Chapel Hill, N.C.: Algonquin Books, 1998), p. 69.
10. Goldsmith, p. 274.
11. Sherna Gluck, ed., *From Parlor to Prison: Five American Suffragists Talk about their Lives*, (New York: Vintage Books, 1976), pp. 65–66.
12. Christine A. Lunardini, *From Equal Suffrage to Equal Rights: Alice Paul and the National Woman's Party, 1910–1928* (New York: New York University Press, 1986), p. 138.
13. Doris Stephens, *Jailed For Freedom*, revised edition, ed. Carol O'Hare (Troutdale, Ore.: New Sage Press, 1995).

Chapter Seven   Women Fight for the Right to Vote

1. Nancy E. McGlen and Karen O'Connor, *Women, Politics, and American Society* (New Jersey: Prentice-Hall, Inc., 1995), p. 118.
2. Ibid.
3. "Women in United States Military History," *Women in Military Service for America Memorial*, n.d., <http://www.womensmemorial.org/historyandcollections/history/learnmoreques.htm> (October 1, 2005).
4. Ibid., p. 2.
5. Judith L. Bellafaire, "The Army Nurse Corps in World War II: A Commemoration of World War II Service," *U.S. Army Center of Military History*, n.d., <http://www.army.mil/cmh-pg/books/wwii/72-14/72-14.htm> (October 4, 2005).
6. "The ERA: A Brief Introduction," *The Equal Rights Amendment*, n.d., <http://www.equalrightsamendment.org/overview.htm> (October 3, 2005).
7. "Margaret Sanger," *Planned Parenthood*, n.d., <http://www.plannedparenthood.org/pp2/portal/files/portal/medicalinfo/birthcontrol/bio-margaret-sanger.xml> (October 5, 2005).
8. "Principal Wars in Which the United States Participated: U.S. Military Personnel and Casualties," *Department of Defense*, n.d., <http://www.dior.whs.mil/mmid/casualty/WCPRINCIPAL.pdf> (November 7, 2005).
9. Blanche Weisen Cook, "Bella Abzug." *Jewish Virtual Library*,

2005, <http://www.jewishvirtuallibrary.org/jsource/biography/abzug> (October 4, 2005).

10. Joel R. Brandes, "History of Divorce in New York," *New York Divorce and Family Law*, n.d., <http://www.brandeslaw.com/grounds_for_divorce/history.htm> (October 1, 2005).

Chapter Eight   Women Try to Expand Their Roles

1. Betty Friedan, *Life So Far* (New York: Simon & Schuster, 2000), p. 142.

2. Ibid., p. 184.

3. "Chronology of the Equal Rights Amendment, 1923–1996," *National Organization for Women*, n.d., <http://www.now.org/issues/economic/cea/history.html> (October 1, 2005).

4. Gloria Steinem, *Moving Beyond Words* (New York: Simon & Schuster, 1994), p. 14.

5. Robin Morgan, ed., *Sisterhood is Powerful* (New York: Random House, 1970), p. 40.

6. Ibid., p. 43.

7. Marcia Cohen, *The Sisterhood: The True Story of the Women Who Changed the World* (New York: Simon & Schuster, 1988), p. 357.

8. N.E.H. Hull and Peter Charles Hoffer, *Roe v. Wade: The Abortion Rights Controversy in American History* (Lawrence: University Press of Kansas, 2001), p. 282.

9. Dorothy and Carl J. Schneider, *Sound Off! American Military Women Speak Out* (New York: E.P. Dutton, 1988), p. 32.

10. Francine D'Amico and Laurie Weinstein, eds., *Gender Camouflage: Women and the U.S. Military* (New York: New York University Press, 1999), p. 52.

11. "The ERA: A Brief Introduction," *The Equal Rights Amendment*, n.d., <http://www.equalrightsamendment.org/overview.htm> (October 3, 2005).

12. Roberta W. Francis, "The History Behind the Equal Rights Amendment," *The Equal Rights Amendment*, n.d., <http://www.equalrightsamendment.org/era.htm> (October 2, 2005).

13. "The Civil Rights Act of 1991," *U.S. Equal Employment Opportunity Commission*, n.d., <www.eeoc.gov/policy/cra91htm> (October 3, 2005).

14. "A Working Woman's Guide to Her Job Rights," U.S. Department of Labor, Elsie Vartanian, Director, August 1992, p. v.

Chapter Nine American Indians Are Forced to Fight

1. *American Indians*, 1996–2005, <http://www.nativeamericans .com> (October 4, 2005).
2. "From 1871 to 1934—Allotment and Assimilation," *A Chronological History of United States Indian Policy and the Indian Response: from 1789 to the Present*, n.d., <http://sorrel.humboldt.edu/~go1/kellogg/Chrono.html> (October 4, 2005).
3. Jack D. Forbes, ed., *The Indian in America's Past* (Englewood Cliffs, N.J.: Prentice-Hall, Inc., 1964), p. 114.
4. Ronald B. Querry, *Native Americans Struggle for Equality* (Vero Beach, Florida: Rourke Corporation, Inc., 1992), p. 43.
5. Oliver La Farge, *As Long as the Grass Shall Grow* (New York: Alliance Book Corporation/Longmans, Green & Company, 1940), pp. 42–44.
6. Forbes, p. 116.
7. John Collier, *Indians of the Americas* (New York: The New American Library, 1948), p. 133.
8. "Today in History: June 2," *American Memory*, n.d., <http://memory.loc.gov/ammem/today/jun02.html> (October 4, 2005).
9. Forbes, p. 118.
10. La Farge, p. 69.
11. James Wilson, *The Earth Shall Weep: A History of Native America* (New York: Atlantic Monthly Press, 1998), p. 364.
12. Alvin M. Josephy, Jr., Joane Nagel, and Troy Johnson, eds., *Red Power: The American Indians' Fight for Freedom* (University of Nebraska Press, 1999), p. 21.
13. Vine Deloria, Jr., and Clifford M. Lytle, *American Indians, American Justice* (Austin, TX: University of Texas Press, 1983), pp. 128-129.
14. Josephy, Jr., Nagel, and Johnson, p. 29.
15. Ibid., p. 39.
16. Ibid., p. 49.
17. Paul Chaat Smith & Robert Allen Warrior, *Like a Hurricane: The Indian Movement from Alcatraz to Wounded Knee* (New York: The New Press, 1996), pp. 270–271.

Chapter Ten Rights for Latinos

1. Carlos M. Fernández-Shaw, *The Hispanic Presence in North America* (New York: Facts on File, 1999), pp. 279–280.
2. "QT-P9. Hispanic or Latino by Type: 2000," *American FactFinder*, n.d., <http://factfinder.census.gov/servlet/QT Table?-geo_id=01000US&-qr_name=DEC_2000_SF1_U QTP9&-ds_name=DEC_2000_SF1_U> (October 3, 2005).

3. Ronald Takaki, *A Different Mirror* (New York: Little, Brown, 1993), p. 178.
4. Rodolfo F. Acuña, *U.S. Latino Issues* (Westport, Conn.: Greenwood Press, 2003), p. 75
5. "QT-P9. Hispanic or Latino by Type: 2000."
6. Ibid.
7. "U.S. Census Bureau Guidance on the Presentation and Comparison of Race and Hispanic Origin Data," *U.S. Census Bureau*, June 12, 2003, <http://www.census.gov/population/www/socdemo/compraceho.html> (Oct. 2, 2005).
8. Takaki, p. 187.
9. Susan Ferriss and Ricardo Sandoval, *The Fight in the Fields: Cesar Chavez and the Farmworkers Movement*, ed. Diana Hembree (New York: Harcourt Brace & Company/ Paradigm, 1997), p. 242.
10. "Address by Cesar Chavez, President, United Farm Workers of America, AFL-CIO, Pacific Lutheran University, March 1989—Tacoma, Washington," *UFW: The Official Web Page of the United Farm Workers of America, AFL-CIO*, n.d., <http://www.ufw.org/fast.htm> (October 3, 2005).
11. Geoffrey Fox, *Hispanic Nation: Culture, Politics, and the Construction of Identity* (Tucson: University of Arizona Press, 1996), p. 163.
12. "Federal Protections Against National Origin Discrimination," *U.S. Department of Justice: Civil Rights Division*, October 2000, <http://www.usdoj.gov/crt/legalinfo/natlorg-cng.htm> (November 7, 2005)
13. Luis C. Moll and Richard Ruiz, "The Schooling of Latino Children," *Latinos: Remaking America*, eds. Marcelo M. Suárez-Orozco and Mariela Páez (Berkeley: University of California Press, 2002), p. 366.
14. Ibid., pp. 26–27.

Chapter Eleven Rights for Asians and People with Disabilities

1. Helen Zia, *Asian American Dreams: The Emergence of an American People* (New York: Farrar, Straus and Giroux, 2000) p. 26.
2. Ronald Takaki, *A Different Mirror* (New York: Little, Brown, 1993), p. 201.
3. "The Chinese Experience: Quiz Answer," *Becoming American: The Chinese Experience*, 2003, <http://www.pbs.org/becomingamerican/ce_quiz2b.html> (October 3, 2005).
4. Ibid.
5. Takaki, p. 206.
6. "This Month in Immigration History," *U.S. Citizenship and*

Immigration Services, n.d., <http://www.uscis.gov/graphics/aboutus/history/dec43.htm> (October 5, 2005).

7. Harry H. L. Kitano, *Japanese Americans: The Evolution of a Subculture* (New Jersey: Prentice-Hall, Inc., 1969), p. 15.

8. Ibid., p. 18.

9. Ibid., p. 31.

10. Takaki, p. 382.

11. Ibid., p. 384.

12. Manning Marable, *The Great Wells of Democracy: The Meaning of Race in American Life* (New York: BasicCivitas Books, 2002), p. 234.

13. "Facts About the Americans with Disabilities Act," *U.S. Equal Opportunity Commission*, January 15, 1997, <http://www.eeoc.gov/facts/fs-ada.html> (October 4, 2005).

14. John Hockenberry, "Yes, You Can", *Parade Magazine*, July 24, 2005, <http://archive.parade.com/2005/0724/0724_disabilities> (September 20, 2005).

15. Ibid.

Chapter Twelve   Have We Overcome?

1. "Women's Earnings Fall; U.S. Census Bureau Finds Rising Gender Wage Gap," *Institute for Women's Policy Research*, August 27, 2004, <http://www.iwpr.org/pdf/WageRatio Press-_release8-27-04.pdf> (November 7, 2005).

2. Ibid.

3. Susan Campbell, "Wisdom Heightens the Value of Voting," *Hartford Courant*, November 5, 2004, p. DI.

4. Darlisa Crawford, "Women Votes in the 2004 Election," *Election Focus 2004*, <http://usinfo.state.gov/dhr/img/assets/5796/elections04_14_043.pdf> (October 2, 2005).

5. Maunel Roig-Franzia, "Vote Reopens Wounds in Alabama," *Hartford Courant*, November 28, 2004, p. B7.

6. Jim Northrup, *The Rez Road Follies: Canoes, Casinos, Computers, and Birch Bark Baskets* (New York: Kodansha America, Inc., 1997), pp. 215–216.

7. "Table A-5. The Population 14 to 24 Years Old by High School Graduate Status . . . ," <http://www.census.gov/population/socdemo/school/tabA-5.xls> (November 7, 2005).

8. Ibid.

9. "Judge Learned Hand," *NACDL E-News*, n.d., <http://www.criminaljustice.org/public.nsf/ENews/2002e67?opendocument> (October 1, 2005).

abolitionist—Person who worked to abolish the slave trade.

act—A name for a law passed by Congress.

advocate—A person who pleads for another person in a court of law. A person who speaks on behalf of some cause.

amendment—A change made in a constitution, a law, or a bill. The U.S. Constitution has twenty-seven amendments. These changes must be approved by two-thirds of the states.

assimilation—To be absorbed into a society.

boycott—When a group of people refuse to buy a product or do business with a company.

civil disobedience—To refuse to obey civil laws. This tactic was used by people to force the laws to be reformed.

demonstration—A planned march or gathering by a group of people. Demonstrations expressed a political point of view.

discrimination—Unfair treatment based on race or gender.

emancipate—To set a group of people free from bondage or slavery.

illiterate—To be unable to read or write; to have little education.

integration—The opening of a school system or other institution to all races.

Memorial to Congress—A statement read before Congress to request the legislators to move forward with a law.

preamble—The introduction to a statute or document. It tells why the document is needed.

ratify—To vote to confirm an amendment or treaty.

reservation—A tract of land set aside for American Indians to use. Reservations were first managed by the federal government.

secession—To withdraw from membership. In America, eleven states withdrew from the Union. This official act, called Secession, was one reason for the Civil War.

segregation laws—Laws that keep a racial or ethnic group separate and apart from the rest of society.

sit-in—An action by a group to occupy a building or place of business peacefully. Sit-ins were used to promote integration or to reform a law.

state militia—A trained group of citizens who serve as soldiers for their state when called upon.

suffrage—The right to vote in a political election.

termination—The removal of an American Indian group from any federal support system.

Books

Aaseng, Nathan. *Cherokee Nation v. Georgia*. San Diego, Calif.: Lucent Books, 2000.

Behnke, Alison. *Chinese in America*. Minneapolis: Lerner Publications Co., 2005.

Crewe, Sabrina, and Dale Anderson. *The Seneca Falls Women's Rights Convention*. Milwaukee, Wis.: G. Stevens Publishing, 2005.

Esherick, Joan. *Guaranteed Rights: The Legislation That Protects Youth With Special Needs*. Broomall, Penn.: Mason Crest Publishers, 2004.

Hurley, Jennifer A., ed. *Women's Rights*. San Diego, Calif.: Greenhaven Press, 2002.

Ingram, Scott. *The 1963 Civil Rights March*. Milwaukee, Wis.: World Almanac Library, 2005.

Kallen, Stuart. *Women of the Civil Rights Movement*. San Diego, Calif.: Lucent Books, 2005.

Karson, Jill. ed. *The Civil Rights Movement*. Farmington Mills, Mich.: Greenhaven Press, 2005.

———. *Leaders of the Civil Rights Movement*. Farmington Hills, Mich.: Greenhaven Press, 2005.

Ochoa, George. *The New York Public Library Amazing Hispanic History: A Book of Answers for Kids*. New York: John Wiley, 1998.

Olson, James S., ed. *Encyclopedia of American Indian Civil Rights*. Westport, Conn.: Greenwood Press, 1997.

Internet Addresses

About Women's History
    <http://womenshistory.about.com>

The Congress of Racial Equality
    <http://www.core-online.org>

The National Association for the Advancement of Colored People
    <http://www.naacp.org>